Advanced Computing Techniques: Implementation, Informatics and Emerging Technologies

(Volume 2)

Digital Transformation in African SMEs: Emerging Issues and Trends

Edited by

Mohammed Majeed
Department of Marketing
Tamale Technical University
Tamale-Ghana

Abdul-Razak Abubakari
Department of Accountancy
Tamale Technical University
Tamale-Ghana

Awini Gideon

Department of Marketing
Tamale Technical University
Tamale-Ghana

&

Jayadatta S.

KLE's Institute of Management Studies (IMSR)
Hubballi, Karnataka 580031
India

Advanced Computing Techniques: Implementation, Informatics and Emerging Technologies

(Volume 2)

Digital Transformation in African SMEs: Emerging Issues and Trends

Editors: Mohammed Majeed, Abdul-Razak Abubakari, Awini Gideon and Jayadatta S.

ISSN (Online): 2737-5730

ISSN (Print): 2737-5722

ISBN (Online): 978-981-5223-34-7

ISBN (Print): 978-981-5223-35-4

ISBN (Paperback): 978-981-5223-36-1

Published by Bentham Science Publishers Pte. Ltd. Singapore. All Rights Reserved.

First published in 2024.

need for a court order if at any point you breach any terms of this License Agreement. In no event will any delay or failure by Bentham Science Publishers in enforcing your compliance with this License Agreement constitute a waiver of any of its rights.

3. You acknowledge that you have read this License Agreement, and agree to be bound by its terms and conditions. To the extent that any other terms and conditions presented on any website of Bentham Science Publishers conflict with, or are inconsistent with, the terms and conditions set out in this License Agreement, you acknowledge that the terms and conditions set out in this License Agreement shall prevail.

Bentham Science Publishers Pte. Ltd.
80 Robinson Road #02-00
Singapore 068898
Singapore
Email: subscriptions@benthamscience.net

BENTHAM SCIENCE

CONTENTS

FOREWORD

Respected reader, you have a treasure in your hands in the name of "*Digital Transformation in African SMEs: Emerging Issues and Trends*". While technological advancements play a role in digital transformation, more technological tools may be even more crucial. Some SMEs are able to complete a digital transformation faster and at much less expense to the firm than others because they have the capacity to build trust in their systems. This book is written for and about digital transformation in Africa. The editors' expertise qualifies them for this good project. They have extensive experience in the field and have spent many years researching the challenges and successes of digital transformation for businesses. Furthermore, they have an intimate understanding of the motivations of these top brass. I agree with the writers that the emphasis should be on technology, people, and performance as the means by which an organization deals with digital disruption. According to my studies, effective digital transformation necessitates adjusting the dynamics of a business and the way its employees perform their duties. There is no sign of a halt to digital disruption any time soon, and it is likely that the typical worker will face multiple waves of disruption over the course of their lifetime. The authors considered digital tools such as social media, Artificial Intelligence, Big Data, IoT, AI, and ML for SMEs. When it comes to relevance, factors influencing the adoption of online shopping and its influence on consumers' intention to shop online are key. The gap between industry leaders and laggards may be rising if these businesses are increasingly reporting and investing time, money, and energy on initiatives to develop these components of their culture. For most SMEs in Africa, I simply believe that changing an organization's leadership, talent, culture, and organization strategy all at once can be a disruptive and inefficient process and that focusing solely on the technological parts of digital transformation is missing out.

Ahmed Tijani
Corporate Affairs & IT
Minerals Commission
Accra – Ghana

PREFACE

In all of Africa's urban centers and rural villages alike, a new breed of digital natives is emerging and poised to stimulate economic development and drive the acceptance of novel digital technologies and services designed to impact all facets of African society and businesses. As a result, the shift to digital is a key factor in the growth and development of resourceful and long-lasting small and medium-sized enterprises. In line with the African Continental Free Trade Area (AfCFTA), the African Union (AU) plans to create a safe and thriving online marketplace in Africa by the year 2030, where people and companies are free to move around and transact online without restriction. Therefore, SMEs in Africa should make use of this unique AU effort to become more tech-savvy, since SNEs' activities, procedures, competencies, and models can all be modernized through digital transformation. Despite this, many African SMEs have not yet fully adopted the digital change in their entire lives. Taking advantage of the digital revolution calls for a shift in perspective, as well as new forms of collaboration between small and medium-sized enterprises (SMEs) and their stakeholders, as well as between different industries. This book is written for business owners and managers of small and medium-sized enterprises (SMEs), with the goal of helping them take advantage of digital technologies and innovation to drive business transformation in Africa and to build and enhance digital networks and services with the end goal of bolstering trade, investment, and capital flows among SMEs. This book will help managers of SMEs discover and enable the digital infrastructure they need to close the digital gap and inequality between themselves and multinational enterprises (MNEs) and to boost distribution and logistics activities that support e-commerce. This book aims to help SMEs in the African market harmonize their environments in order to guarantee cheaper customer service, expand their reach, and secure more funding to help them close the digital infrastructure gap and achieve a universally accessible market, affordable prices, and secure e-commerce. Last but not least, African SMEs need to learn to embrace the adaptability of their business models, identify their greatest threats, and devise strategies to turn those threats into chances for growth. SMEs in Africa stand to gain valuable insights that will enable them to better locate and exploit new business possibilities presented by digital transformation. The book is compiled based on African SMEs, with contributors from around the globe (*e.g.* India, Australia, and Ghana). The book covers digital transformation tools such as e-commerce, social media, Big Data, the Internet of Things, Artificial Intelligence, Machine learning, online shopping and digitization initiatives.

Mohammed Majeed
Department of Marketing
Tamale Technical University
Tamale-Ghana

Awini Gideon
Department of Marketing
Tamale Technical University
Tamale-Ghana

Abdul-Razak Abubakari
Department of Accountancy
Tamale Technical University
Tamale-Ghana

&

Jayadatta S.
KLE's Institute of Management Studies (IMSR)
Hubballi, Karnataka 580031
India

List of Contributors

Abas S.	Tamale Technical University, Tamale, Ghana
Ahmed Tijani	Minerals Commission, Tamale, Northern Region, Ghana
Aloriwor Elijah Kutogichiga	Department of Social Studies, Tamale Islamic Science Senior High School, Tamale, Ghana
Alhassan Fatawu	Tamale Technical University, Tamale-Ghana
Ashmond Adu-Ansere	Akenten Appiah Menka University of Skills, Training, and Entrepreneurial Development, Mampong, Ghana
Asare Charles	Ghana Communication Technology University, Tamale, Northern Region, Ghana
Felli Gideon Kupule Adobauru	C. K. Tedam University of Technology and Applied Sciences, Navrongo, Ghana
Awini Gideon	Department of Marketing, Tamale Technical University, Tamale-Ghana
Jayadatta S.	KLE's Institute of Management Studies (IMSR), Hubballi, Karnataka 580031, India
Kobby Mensah	University of Ghana, Legon-Ghana
Mohammed Majeed	Department of Marketing, Tamale Technical University, Tamale-Ghana
Nana Arko-Cole	University of Professional Studies, Accra, Tamale, Northern Region, Ghana
Nkayi Kwasi	Tamale Teaching Hospital, Salaga/yendi Rd, Tamale, Ghana
Parag Shukla	Department of Commerce, and Business Management, Faculty of Commerce The Maharaja Sayajirao University of Baroda, Pratapgunj, Vadodara, Gujarat-390002, India
Sophia Jonathan Machemba	The Maharaja Sayajirao University of Baroda, Pratapgunj, Vadodara, Gujarat-390002, India
Stephen Mahama Braimah	University of Ghana, Legon-Ghana
Stanley C.	Tamale Technical University, Tamale-Ghana
Susana A.	Accra Technical University, Accra-Ghana
Victus Elikplim Lumorvie	Lanzhou University of Technology, Lanzhou-Gansu Province, Lanzhou, China
Yomboi Jonas	St. John's Integrated Senior High/Tech. School – Navrongo, Ghana
Zakari Bukari	University of Professional Studies, Accra-Ghana

CHAPTER 1

Digital Tools (Big Data, IoT, AI, ML, *etc.*) for SMEs

Ashmond Adu-Ansere[1,*] and **Victus Elikplim Lumorvie**[2]

[1] *Akenten Appiah Menka University of Skills, Training, and Entrepreneurial Development, Mampong, Ghana*

[2] *Lanzhou University of Technology, Lanzhou-Gansu Province, Lanzhou, China*

Abstract: This article discusses the significance of artificial intelligence (AI) and machine learning (ML) for small and medium-sized enterprises (SMEs) and the challenges that hinder their adoption in Africa and other developing countries. Despite the success of AI and ML in improving performance and productivity in large organizations, many SMEs are reluctant to adopt these digital tools due to a lack of awareness and education. The article highlights the benefits of AI and ML for SMEs, including better decision-making, increased productivity, revenue generation, and innovation. It also discusses how AI and ML can be used for customer service, marketing, and sales automation, and emphasizes the need for SMEs to embrace these technologies to improve their competitiveness in the market.

Keywords: Adoption, Artificial intelligence, Challenges, Machine learning, SMEs.

INTRODUCTION

The advent of digital technologies has impacted the novelty and efficiency of businesses immensely [1 - 3]. This trend has become a revolution that has taken global interactions, businesses, and transactions by storm as it influences connectivity, introduces new procedures, and enhances performance [2, 4]. Digitalization and its associated applications are disrupting several sectors and industries and threaten to make existing models and ways of doing things obsolete by introducing new trends [3, 5]. The influx and expeditious adoption of digitalization have transformed organizational and inter-organizational practices, value chains, and industrial competitiveness [3, 6]. The digitalization process involves digital tools such as the *Internet of Things* (IoT), *artificial intelligence* (AI), *machine learning* (ML), *the Internet of People* (IoP), *the Internet of Energy*

* **Corresponding author Ashmond Adu-Ansere:** Akenten Appiah Menka University of Skills, Training, and Entrepreneurial Development, Mampong, Ghana; E-mail: ashmonda@gmail.com

Mohammed Majeed, Abdul-Razak Abubakari, Awini Gideon and Jayadatta S. (Eds.)

(IoE), and several others that are adopted by firms to manage their operations, carry out strategies, and to gain competitive advantage [7 - 9]. Research hasexamined the nexus between these digital tools and business performance and varied outcomes report strong and positive effects, negative effects, and others contend that these tools undermine performance [4, 7, 10, 11]. Although the adoption of these digital tools propels SMEs to be competitive both locally and globally, the majority of these SMEs are lagging in terms of digital evolution.

Small and medium-scale enterprises are motivated to adopt digitalization to achieve internal efficiencies, collaborate effectively with partners, reduce costs, introduce new offerings to satisfy needs, gather intelligence, and create employment opportunities [12, 13]. Rahayu and Day [14] posit that these tools help SMEs to become more effective, efficient, innovative, and expansive to rub shoulders with their larger competitors in the global market [7,15–17]. Thus, SMEs that use these digital tools are more likely to outwit their competitors because they expedite future research, strategic planning, and business forecasting, resulting in organizational flexibility [18, 19]. Tarutèa and Gatautisa [15] in their study observed that the adoption of these tools impacts profitability, growth, satisfaction, social and environmental performance, and value. In this light, the effect of these digital tools on the activities of SMEs in Africa can never be overemphasized.

Small and Medium-scale Enterprises (SMEs)

The contribution of small and medium enterprises (SMEs) cannot be overemphasized as they impact economic growth, global market competitiveness, national development, poverty alleviation, employment generation, and innovation commercialization [14, 15, 18, 20]. Largely, they contribute immensely to the increasing gross domestic product, new business creation, and income generation [14, 21]. Regarding employment in developed economies such as the United Kingdom, Germany, and the United States, SMEs employ nearly 99 per cent of the workforce and contribute roughly 70 per cent of the national GDP is mostly around 70 per cent [22, 23]. However, in developing nations such as Ghana, Togo, and Nigeria, their contribution to GDP hovers around 50 percent, and are private businesses dominant [14, 21]. It can therefore be interpreted that SMEs form the backbone of the global economy.

Contexts cannot be overlooked in the definition of SMEs because of the variations in economies, and the sectors that constitute the economies. As a result, the definition and classification of SMEs differ among continents, regions, and countries. Thus, no generally accepted definition and classification exist for SMEs. The parameters for classifying SMEs involve the number of employees, sales turnover, customer base, available plant and machinery, annual turnover, and several others. In developed economies like the UK, USA, and Germany, small and medium-scale enterprises are classified based on the number of employees and turnover, in that the EU sets the limit at 250 employees and an annual turnover of around Euro, and other bodies consider institutions with 50 million Euro revenue and less than 500 employees. In developing economies such as the African regions, businesses with employees from 1 to 200 or 300 are all considered SMEs [24, 25].

Small and Medium-scale Enterprises in Africa

Small and medium-scale enterprises SMEs in Africa constitute about ninety [90] per cent of private businesses, employ more than fifty [50] per cent of the working class, and contribute grossly to the gross domestic product (GDP) of the nations [14, 26, 27]. Specifically in Nigeria, SMEs are the primary source of employment and comprise more than 90 per cent of businesses in the country [17]. Similarly, in other developing countries like Ghana, SMEs are pivotal to innovation, job creation national development, and growth as they contribute approximately 70 to GDP and constitute over 90 per cent of businesses [15, 28]. In as much as these SMEs remain the driving force of the economies of these developing countries in Africa, their rate of adoption for digitalization is very low compared to their counterparts in the developed economies [14]. This in turn stifles their global competitiveness and slows down their rate of growth considering that digitalization is at the heart of efficiency and productivity that leads to achieving competitive advantage and improving overall performance [14, 26, 28 - 30]. Leaders of SMEs in these nations are gradually prioritizing the adoption of these digital tools through information technology to achieve efficiency, enhance product innovation, make effective decisions, explore opportunities, mitigate threats, and gain competitive advantage [26, 28, 29].

DIGITAL TOOLS FOR SMES

Small and medium-scale enterprises (SMEs) adopt several digital tools for diverse reasons in their activities. Some of these digital tools are discussed below.

Big Data

Big data is ubiquitous to this generation as its tenets keep spreading like wildfire in a dry season. It is a pivotal digital tool adopted by SMEs in this era of data ubiquity. This age is data-driven, as both structured and unstructured facts are sourced from diverse spheres to help individuals and entities make informed decisions. Research predicts that the global big data market will rise from $193.14 billion to about $420.98 billion by 2027 and the emergence of big data will remain an inviolable phenomenon that cannot be overemphasized as the daily data generation is estimated at 2.5 quintillion bytes in the past few decades (Borasi *et al.*, 2020; Olabode *et al.*, 2022).

About Big Data

Big data has garnered enormous attention globally in the past decades from diverse fields and disciplines such as supply chain [30], marketing [31], healthcare [32, 33], information technology, construction, hospitality [31, 34], and several others. It is considered the new era of transformation in terms of data collection and usage for major disciplines and businesses. As its dominance intensifies with time [35], ambiguity still surrounds its evolution and application as some practitioners argue that it is not entirely a new trend and make reference to the US census as far back as the 1880s where the classification and reporting of information on approximately 50 million individuals became a daunting task for the analysts of the time [36]. One may strongly contest that the amount of information contained in that census will no longer be considered big data in this era where technology is far advanced but that could open up contextual arguments regarding the definitions of the concept [37 - 40].

Research has defined big data from different perspectives and contexts and its popularity has been attributed to the extensive usage of mobile devices and other social media platforms [35]. Big data has been defined as data that stem from diverse channels such as sensors, and social media platforms: photo and video uploads, satellites, mobile devices, and GPS signals. Thus, it includes large data sets, technologies, and amounts of data from a variety of sources, ranging from Web click stream data to genomic and proteomic data from scientific research, and consumer behaviour. Other scholars define 'big data as data that is too voluminous or huge to be handled and transformed by traditional analytical approaches *via* a typical database software and stored in an organizational data mart and warehouse. Such data cannot be processed and loaded easily into computer memory for future retrieval and its components are the data itself, the process involved in analysing it- which has information technology (IT) and algorithm at heart to identify patterns, and the mode of presentation of the results that could inform insightful decision making. Explicitly, big data is defined as "the ability of a firm to effectively deploy technology and talent to capture, store and analyze data, toward the generation of insight" [38]. This includes the techniques and online technologies that are employed to generate large amounts of facts from varied sources for analysis and interpretation that traditional procedures can neither handle nor execute to make insightful decisions.

Another school of thought defines 'big data' from the 'V' perspective which began with the three 'Vs' of Volume, Velocity, and Variety. The 'Volume' of big data describes its size and the storage capacity needed to preserve it for later retrieval. Big data is a voluminous set of data in terms of the number of records it contains and the amount of space required to save and process it into meaningful information. Brands like Tesco, Walmart, Jumia, Amazon, Microsoft, and Apple generate billions of items on daily and weekly basis, petabytes of information, and quintillion bytes of records. The persistent increase in high data volume generated can be associated with the advancement in technology and internet connectivity, and customers' willingness to share information [40]. The 'Variety' of big data explains the fact it could be unstructured, semi-structured, or structured, gathered from multiple sources comprising primary or secondary (surveys, interviews, focus groups, customer databases, and loyalty schemes) but integrated to serve its intended purpose [40]. Therefore, organizations with the capacity and ability to source data from different platforms can triangulate the results and make strategic decisions. With the advent of big data, facts can be gathered from diverse sources such as social media platforms, search engines such as Google, GPS, censuses, and many more. The third 'V' that stands for velocity indicates the speed at which these facts are generated and delivered. Velocity in this context could also refer to the state of obsolescence that occurs within the data collection, transformation, and presentation period. If 'big', then it is expected to stand the test of time to drive organizational agility and performance.

This 'V' concept evolved and two additions, 'veracity' and 'value' were proposed to better explain the conversation of 'big data' by other scholars. The veracity component of 'big data' highlights how trustworthy and of high-quality the data is to make accurate predictions. Businesses are mostly bombarded with data duplication issues and it is criticized that if the data touted as 'big', and is full of replications, then the credibility of the data is questionable. Value for data considers the ability of the big data to generate economically worthy insights and or benefits from the extracted data. Thus, the huge amount of data should produce prised insights and results [35, 38, 40]. Additionally, scholars have advanced the conversation by proposing 'Variability' and 'Visualisation' as other attributes of 'big data [39]. Variability in this context refers to the inconsistencies associated with huge amounts of data due to their sources, contexts, the technology and analytics adopted, and the methods of analysis that could influence its results and interpretation. The focus is to triangulate to mitigate information asymmetry and discrepancies. The seventh 'V', Visualization describes the ability to interpret data to gain understanding. However, the size, speed, value, and variety of 'big data' impels the adoption of new technologies to manage and process its features because the traditional data-processing infrastructure cannot handle them [33, 41]. In this chapter, Big Data is defined as the phenomenon that requires specific technologies in the collection and management of facts with high velocity, variability, value, volume, veracity, and from numerous sources to make strategic decisions.

The concept of Big Data has become a phenomenon and not a mere technology [13, 33], with much emphasis placed on the processes involved in creating value from it rather than magnifying its volume and availability.

Big Data Analytics

Research has argued that acquiring voluminous data from many sources with high velocity and variability will amount to nothing without constructive analytical processing and interpretation [42]. This explains that the existence of the data does not guarantee relevant knowledge generation that can improve performance and produce a competitive advantage [35, 39, 43]. Data analytics as a broad concept involves the process of accessing, storing, analyzing, and interpreting data to achieve meaningful insights [30, 42, 44]. This involves the discovery of complex patterns of relationships within a large amount of data through approaches such as text analytics, web analytics, mobile analytics, network analytics, and other techniques by leveraging advanced technological accessibility to drive strategic actions [45, 46]. Research has indicated that several organizations are failing to realize and utilize the full potential of the existence of big data and the phenomenon sometimes becomes a curse rather than a blessing to such organizations due to the lack of knowledge and technical abilities to handle and manage such large raw facts [47]. Careful execution of big data analytics helps organizations to transform this bulky data into meaningful information that could improve strategic decision-making and enhance organizational performance. Some researchers consider BDA as the next breakthrough that could benchmark efficiency, innovativeness, and great competitive advantage. In this context, big data analytics can be defined as the new trend of extracting meaningful information from large and unstructured facts parsimoniously and swiftly from diverse sources with the help of technology to inform current and future decisions [38, 48]. Existing studies have proposed that the big data analytics process involves five key steps which include data acquisition and recording, data extraction/cleaning/annotation, data integration/aggregation/ representation, data analysis/modelling, and the interpretation of results. This is a systematic process that organizations follow to transform a high volume of complex data into meaningful insight.

Acquisition and Recording of Data

The first step, data acquisition and recording, specifies the facts that must be gathered, the sources from which they may be gathered, and the methods for gathering. It is prudent to specify the information requirements to employ the right tool and approach that can collect and record the data at the desired volume swiftly and accurately without losing its value.

Information Extraction/Cleaning/Annotation

After gathering the information, the next essential step is to whittle it down to workable units because the data in its raw state will not be in a suitable format for analysis. For example, large data gathered from a social media site will contain several conflicting and irrelevant details. As a result, leaving the data in this format will hinder effective analysis and that will influence the results. So, the data is subjected to social media analytics- an information extraction process to draw the desired patterns from the big pool into a structured form suitable for analysis.

Data Integration, Aggregation, and Representation

Big data is gathered from multiple sources and in reality, replications will occur among the data deposited in various warehouses which will make it difficult for users to navigate through such data. For instance, consumer data may be gathered from social media platforms such as Twitter, Facebook, YouTube, and WhatsApp. Triangulation of such data will help curb issues of duplication and also compare results. However, depending on the situation at hand, one source or design will be preferred to the other. A substantial body of work at the data integration stage can curb several challenges during the analysis of the data, in that, differences in data structure and semantics ought to be expressed in computer-comprehensible forms to help realise automated error-free difference resolutions.

Analysis/Modeling

The techniques employed in the quizzing, mining, and analysis of Big data differ significantly from standard statistical analysis of small data. Although Big data is frequently touted as noisy, dynamic, diverse, linked, and unreliable, it is argued that generic statistics derived from frequent patterns and correlation analyses typically outclass individual fluxes and often reveal more reliable underlying patterns and information that make even a noisy Big data more useful than small data. Nonetheless, data mining techniques can be applied to big data to improve its quality and reliability for a better understanding of the underlying semantics and provide intelligent querying functions.

Interpretation

What makes Big data relevant is the ability to interpret and make meaning of the analysed data or the big data is of limited value. Decision-makers will rely on supplementary information, also called the provenance of the result- that demystifies the complex process and the results derived to make informed decisions. This process makes it possible for all users not only to interpret the results but to also replicate the analysis in different contexts, with diverse assumptions, and data sets.

Big Data Techniques

The distinct attributes of Big Data require specified applications, and extraordinary techniques to proficiently transform voluminous data into meaningful information at a specified time. Various institutions such as Amazon, eBay, and Walmart adopt diverse techniques to extract and explore patterns from bulky transactional data to make strategic decisions that could translate into achieving competitive advantage. Successful BDA techniques integrate overlapping activities from diverse fields such as statistics, machine learning, signal processing, social network analysis, data mining, Artificial Intelligence, and visualization approaches.

Statistics

Statistics primarily involves the science of collecting, organizing, and interpreting data. Large numerical data is meaningful until statistical methods are applied to examine relationships (causal, or/and correlation) between objects. Nonetheless, it is contended that regular statistical techniques are unsuitable to manage big data. Hence, the call for advanced versions or completely new approaches.

Data Mining

Data mining constitutes a set of techniques such as regression, clustering analysis, and several others used to extract valuable information (patterns) from data. It is aimed at discovering previously unknown patterns to be used in making decisions that could impact the future of businesses. This does not involve the extraction of the data itself but the patterns that exist in the data. The three major techniques involved in data mining are exploration, pattern identification, and deployment. *Exploration*: at the explorations stage, the data is cleaned and transformed into another form, and essential variables are determined. This is followed by *Pattern Identification*: where the patterns which make the best prediction are identified and selected. *Deployment*: finally, the identified patterns are arrayed for the desired outcome.

Machine Learning

Machine learning is an essential technique aimed to design algorithms that allow computers to evolve behaviours based on empirical data. Primarily, machine learning is employed to discover knowledge and make intelligent decisions automatically. In the context of Big Data, machine learning algorithms are scaled up to cope with the data. There exist a wide array of scale machine learning algorithms, but many important specific sub-fields in large-scale machine learning, such as large-scale recommender systems, natural language processing, association rule learning, and ensemble learning still face scalability problems.

Optimization Methods

The optimization method is another technique widely adopted to solve quantitative problems in diverse fields, predominantly in the natural sciences-physics, biology, engineering, and economics. Many Big Data applications, such as WSNs and ITSs, require real-time optimization. Alternative approaches to optimization problems include data reduction and parallelization. Numerous computational strategies for dealing with global optimization problems exist, including simulated annealing, adaptive simulated annealing, and quantum annealing, as well as a genetic algorithm that naturally lends itself to parallelism and can thus be highly efficient.

Social Network Analysis (SNA)

This technique has gained popularity in sociology, anthropology, biology, economics, history, social psychology, and many other disciplines. It examines social relationships in terms of network theory and is often considered a consumer tool as it constitutes social system design, human behaviour modelling, social network visualization, social network evolution analysis, and graph query and mining. Applying this technique in big data transformation is quite a daunting task so social, and cloud computing are mostly the preferred options.

Visualization

The visualization technique, as the name implies is employed to create and project images, diagrams, tables, and other innate demonstrations to help appreciate the data. Unlike traditional data that is small and easy to handle, the complexity of Big Data poses a challenge to its visualization. As a result, before the actual data interpretation, most researchers use geometric modelling and feature extraction to significantly reduce the data size. It is noteworthy that the choice of a proper data representation is central to the visualization of big data.

Influence of Big Data on SMEs

Several SMEs from diverse fields such as healthcare, hospitality, tourism, supply chain, automotive, retail, clothing, pharmaceutical, and finance are adopting Big Data to adapt to the dynamic business environment and increase performance, efficiency, and productivity [42, 49, 50]. Most global and international companies like Netflix, Tonaton, Amazon, DHL, American Express, and Starbucks have largely integrated BDA into their operation but its adoption in SMEs is still at the infancy stage globally [4, 14, 51]. In reality, sectors such as banking rely on big data to examine financial trends and also measure the satisfaction and loyalty of their customers. Malls and supermarkets on the other hand can determine customer preferences, and promote and customize their offerings to suit customers' preferences [50, 51].

Research has established the need for SMEs to adopt BDA in organizations to enhance innovativeness, product development, and forecasting which could lead to gaining a competitive advantage. SMEs that stagger in their adoption will be lagging in growth compared to larger organizations. Although most of these SMEs desire to implement BDA in their system, its adoption is not without challenges [51, 52]. These challenges hinder the adoption of Big Data in SMEs and notable among them include the lack of IT infrastructure, data security issues, economic/financial constraints, and unskilled staff.

Lack of IT Infrastructure

The inadequacy and lack of IT infrastructure is a major challenge for SMEs in their quest for Big Data adoption because an advanced and accurate IT system is pivotal to the utilization of BDA [50, 53]. Sadly, most of these SMEs operate basic IT infrastructure systems that cannot process Big Data analytics [38, 54].

Data Security Issues

Data security is of much concern as data availability and this poses a great challenge to SMEs as no established standards and regulations guide the usage and ethics of BDA [51]. SMEs are more exposed to this threat because of the porous nature of their system, and the outdated security software database management systems that can be easily hacked.

Financial Constraints/Economic

Most of these tools are very expensive to acquire and manage. The cost of investing in technology are a big constrain amongst SMEs in Africa [51]. However, many of these SMEs are handicapped regarding their acquisition because of the limited financial resources available to them. As a result, SMEs especially those in developing countries are sceptical about investing in the sophisticated and advanced functions of BDA which are very expensive [51, 55].

Unskilled Staff

SMEs are confronted with another challenge of unskilled and inexperienced IT specialists handling BDA activities [55]. The tenets of Big Data hold that Big Data is associated with big impacts so if not well managed, the anticipated blessings will turn into curses. Most SMEs have few or no permanent skilled IT staff such as data scientists, programmers, or analysts to handle the technicalities associated with Big Data [6, 51]. This makes it difficult for SMEs to adopt and implement big data as a digital tool compared to big organizations that have a pool of talents with the technical know-how to choose from, the financial muscle, up-to-date security systems, and reliable IT infrastructure.

INTERNET OF THINGS (IOT)

With the rapid growth of technology and digitalization, the Internet of Things (IoT) has evolved into a vital digital tool that has gained prominence in both industrial and academic fields in recent times, and the globally connected technological devices (gadgets) are projected to reach 6.5 billion units by the year 2025 [56]. The Internet of Things (IoT) is a newly discovered paradigm that integrates the Internet and many heterogeneous physical objects enabling numerous innovative applications in different domains such as logistics, industrial processes, public safety, home automation, environmental monitoring, and health care. The Internet of Things (IoT) is a technical trend that allows humans to communicate with information and communication technologies (ICT) at any time and from any location while also meeting security and privacy criteria.

Currently, due to the heterogeneous nature of IoT, a wide range of multimedia physical objects have been connected to the internet. Marjani *et al.* [57] recounted that, a significant increase in multimedia big data generated from IoT devices, where this volume increases with the diminishing size and mobile nature of IoT devices. Furthermore, IoT cannot only sense things but can also control and actuate things, and connect, and exchange data over the Internet [58, 59]. Meanwhile, by 2025, approximately 2-3 billion people will access the internet also economic growth caused by IoT is estimated to be in the range of $2.7 trillion to $6.2 trillion [30, 59]. In addition, the percent of economic growth in the various application arenas caused by deploying IoT in medical care, manufacturing, electricity, metropolitan infrastructure, safety, resource extortion agriculture, vehicles, and retail is 41%, 33%, 7%, 4%, 4%, 4%, 2%, and 1% respectively.

As shown in Fig. (**1**), IoT typically has three layers of architecture consisting of Perception, Network, and Application layers [59].

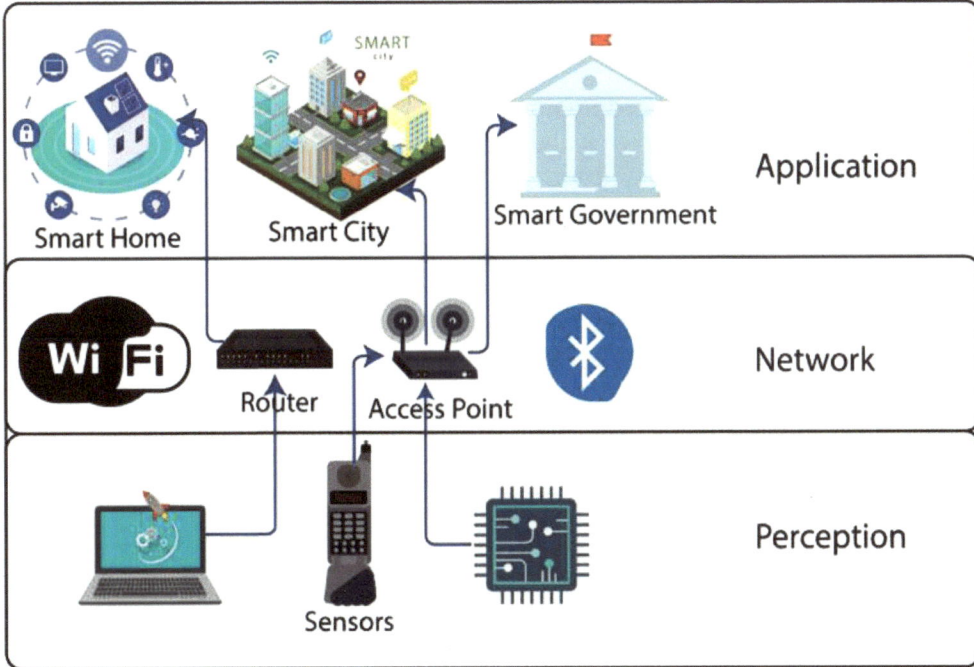

Fig. (1). The 3-architecture layer of the internet of things.

Perception Layer

Its main objectives are to connect things to the IoT network, and to measure, collect, and process the state information associated with these things *via* deployed smart devices, transmitting the processed information into the upper layer *via* layer interfaces [60].

Network Layer

This layer is also referred to as the transportation layer. The network layer is used to receive the processed information provided by the perception layer and determine the routes to transmit the data and information to the IoT hub, devices, and applications *via* integrated networks [60]. The network layer is the most important in IoT architecture, because various devices (hub, switching, gateway, cloud computing perform, *etc.*), and various communication technologies (Bluetooth, Wi-Fi, long-term evolution, *etc.*) are integrated into this layer.

Application (Service) Layer

The application layer receives the data transmitted from the network layer and uses the data to provide required services or operations. Many applications exist in this layer, each having different requirements [60].

Several mobile devices are been integrated into the internet due to their ubiquitous nature enabling advanced services and applications based on human-to-device and device to devices in physical and virtual environments. These multimedia devices can be cameras, smart refrigerators, smart cars, smart air conditioners, printers, smart tablets, *etc.* as shown in Fig. (**2**) harvesting the multimedia information from smart environments and reporting to administrators. The multimedia information harvested from these multimedia devices could be in different forms video files, audio files, text files, graphics, *etc.*

The Multimedia Internet of Things architecture can be seen in Fig. (**2**) integrating diverse multimedia smart devices, gateway, control Centre, users, and storage server.

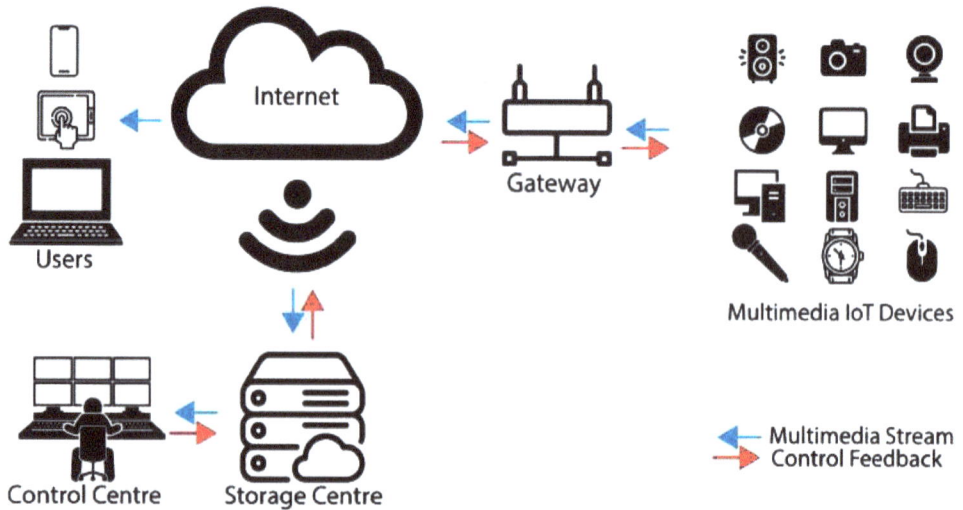

Fig. (2). Architecture of multimedia internet of things.

Intrusion Detection in IoT

As technology evolves over the years and a lot of multimedia objects such as smartphones, small refrigerators, security cameras, *etc.* are connected to the internet, the main focus of network security in combating attacks has been to protect digital information by maintaining data confidentiality, integrity and also ensuring the availability of resources when needed [60, 61]. This as a result has attracted researchers at home and abroad to intensively use both traditional network security methods called Firewall Technology and Intrusion Detection systems to defend against these kinds of attacks in the Multimedia Internet of Things.

Meanwhile, current research within the scope of IoT uses machine learning-based IDS methods for detecting unauthorized users in IoT networks. Instances of these mainly used approaches are; SVM, Naïve Bayes, Deep learning, Decision Tree, Genetic algorithms, neural networks [60, 62], and several others.

Information transmitted and the privacy of individuals are one essential area continuously researched and the need for security to be enhanced. Shifa *et al.* [63] opine that, although IoT merges the physical world and the online world, it is not without risk. This is because every message that is sent or received from such smart objects in an IoT environment normally passes through several nodes to reach their destination and they use heterogeneous communication technologies, devices, and protocols hence making these messages prone to interception attacks. It is further argued that the prevalence of many connected devices, heterogeneous protocols, and platforms creates many new security challenges in terms of privacy, confidentiality, authentication, access control, and trust [30].

IoT for SMEs

IoT as a digital tool infers ubiquitous systems that propel SMEs to operate digitally and remain competitive through the gathering and analysis of data from multiple sources to make informed decisions [64]. Its adoption requires efficient and sophisticated networking, hardware, and software technologies to execute projects that meet existing and future customer needs [65, 66]. In this light, most SMEs are unable to attain the full potential of IoT because of the associated costs so they succumb to the dominance of their competitors. It is perceived that digital tools such as IoT are meant for large organizations. Nonetheless, there are affordable IoT applications that can be employed by SMEs to increase productivity, monitor and control operations, and improve performance [67, 68]. These IoT systems help organizations in the collection of data to make strategic decisions, customize offerings to suit consumers' preferences, build long-term relationships with customers, and generate innovative ideas that give a competitive advantage [10, 69]. Atzori *et al.* proposed some examples of IoT technologies that SMEs could employ to gain competitive advantage and they include tracking system of products in real-time *via radio-frequency Identification* (RFID), *wireless sensor networks* (WSNs) for monitoring environmental factors such as temperature and humidity to improve the efficiency of the food supply chain and comfortable offices for employees equipped with monitoring and alarm systems, *middleware, cloud computing*, and *IoT applications software.*

To ascertain whether SMEs are ready to adopt IoT as a digital tool, some internal and external factors ought to be considered [15, 70]. First, is access to broadband internet technologies because these systems rely on internet connectivity to function effectively [71]. It is noteworthy that it is one thing to set up the edifice, and another thing for it to run efficiently to produce the desired results [72]. Thus, it requires the integration of the mechanics and the dynamics to achieve IoT success. Secondly, the size of the firm and limited economic resources will also determine its readiness and ability to adopt IoT technologies [28, 73, 74]. The installation and set-up of these devices are mostly capital-intensive so smaller firms usually are at a disadvantage because they may lack the financial capacity to implement them even though their benefits cannot be undermined. Additionally, the technological skills and leadership perception of investment in digital technologies are essential factors that cannot be underestimated [75, 76]. When the organization lacks competent technical staff, and the leadership is not technologically oriented, the benefits associated with IoT technologies will be overlooked and such organizations will be lagging in the competitive and dynamic environment. Importantly, the lack of security and privacy of information assets could hinder the execution and implementation of IoT technologies [74]. Confidentiality and information security are of great concern to customers so they demand high protection of their details and would not be aligned with institutions with porous security systems that may be prone to potential attacks. The final condition is the legalities and regulations surrounding IoT [75, 77]. Although the system is ubiquitous and friendly, some legal and regulatory obligations ought to be met to operate successfully. Flouting these measures could trigger severe consequences. Enterprises should first be aware of the existing requirements and take the required steps to meet them. While larger establishments may have a whole legal department to handle such issues, SMEs may struggle to meet such conditions.

STAGES INVOLVED IN EXECUTING IOT PROJECTS IN SMES

Prior studies have outlined procedures to be followed by small and medium-scale enterprises (SMEs) that plan to adopt IoT solutions [78]. They include:

- *Understanding the IoT ecosystem*
- *Defining the IoT-related business objectives*
- *Setting the business strategy*
- *Deployment of technological infrastructure*
- *Acquisition of cloud technology*

- *Hiring and training staff*
- *Hiring external IoT providers*
- *Addressing concerns related to security vulnerability*

The are several benefits attributed to the adoption of IoT solutions as a digital tool in SMEs [64]. Enterprises that implement e-commerce can enhance their deliveries through IoT technologies deployment to track goods in real-time to reduce management's costs, reduce the risk of customer deception by producing quality, confirm customers' orders by providing shopping carts, and several others [79].

Previous studies have examined the interplay of IoT and SMEs. Parra-Sanchez *et al.* assessed ICT policies for digital transformation in Colombia and the technology readiness for IoT adoption in SMEs in the trading sector and highlighted that technology readiness is crucial for adopting technological trends. In their study, they recount that although SMEs have technological and economic limitations for adopting IoT, some defy all odds to venture into IoT solutions adoption to create IoT-based services [56, 80].

In another study, Vermanen, Rantanen, and Harkke investigate the ethical issues related to the Internet of Things (IoT) deployment in small- and medium-sized enterprises SMEs by applying Mason's original privacy, accuracy, property, and accessibility (PAPA) framework [81]. It is revealed that while the original PAPA framework can serve as a generic ethical appraisal tool, it lacks the coverage of several IoT-specific issue areas. As a result, two new categories were developed-motivation and security to meticulously address the ethical risks associated with IoT. Thus, SMEs ought to be guarded in their implementation of IoT solutions by taking into consideration all ethical risk factors.

Leminen, Rajahonka, Westerlund, and Wendelin assessed the future of the Internet of Things toward hierarchical ecosystems and service business models to answer two key research questions: What are the different types of IoT business models; and how do these identified models emerge [82]? Building on a systematic literature review of IoT ecosystems and business models, they identified four types of IoT business models: value chain efficiency, industry collaboration, horizontal market, and platform. SMEs that adopt IoT in their activities are likely to implement one or more of these categories to enhance their operations and attain the full potential of IoT.

It is projected that the Internet of Things (IoT) would play a central role in the everyday life and interactions of individuals and organizations because it integrates varied systems and things from different backgrounds with an enormous potential for reduced costs due to better adeptness and practices [83].

As such, companies can easily manage industrial processes by linking the physical and digital worlds to develop new offerings for their customers *via* the data collected from diverse objects, devices, and machines to deliver value in monitoring, control, optimization, and autonomy [84].

ARTIFICIAL INTELLIGENCE (AI), MACHINE LEARNING (ML), AND DEEP LEARNING (DL)

Artificial Intelligence is the field of developing computers and robots to mimic human cognitive functions such as learning and problem-solving beyond human capabilities. AI-enabled programs can analyze and contextualize data to provide information or automatically trigger actions without human interference [85]. Currently, AI is at the centre of many modern technologies that have been deployed in several areas to make life easy. To be thriving in nearly any industry, where SMEs are not an exception, organizations must be able to transform their data into actionable insight to make timely data-driven decisions with greater speed and efficiency. AI and ML give the organization the advantage of automating a variety of manual processes involving data and decision-making.

Machine Learning, on the other hand, refers to the technologies and algorithms that enable systems to identify patterns, make decisions, and improve themselves through experience and data. ML is an application or subset of AI that enables computer systems to make predictions or take decisions using historical data without being programmed explicitly. It is the process of using mathematical models of data to help a computer learn without direct instruction, hence enabling a computer system to continue learning and improving on its own based on experience. They are often used interchangeably [86]. Fortune Business Insight stated that the global machine learning sector is expected to grow from US$15.50 billion in 2021 to US$152.24 billion in 2028, with an annual growth rate of 38.6%.

The machine learning techniques are categorized into three main types; supervised, unsupervised and semi-supervised machine learning. The most commonly used machine learning algorithms include Support Vector Machine (SVM), Decision Tree, Artificial Neural Network (ANN), Random Forests (RF), Naïve Bayes, K-means clustering, Genetic Algorithm, *etc*. The following Fig. (3) shows the generic architecture of machine learning techniques used in this thesis.

As shown in Fig. (3), supervised learning is when the model is getting trained on a labelled dataset. The labelled dataset has both input and output parameters. Classification and Regression are the two main simple classic algorithms in Supervised Learning.

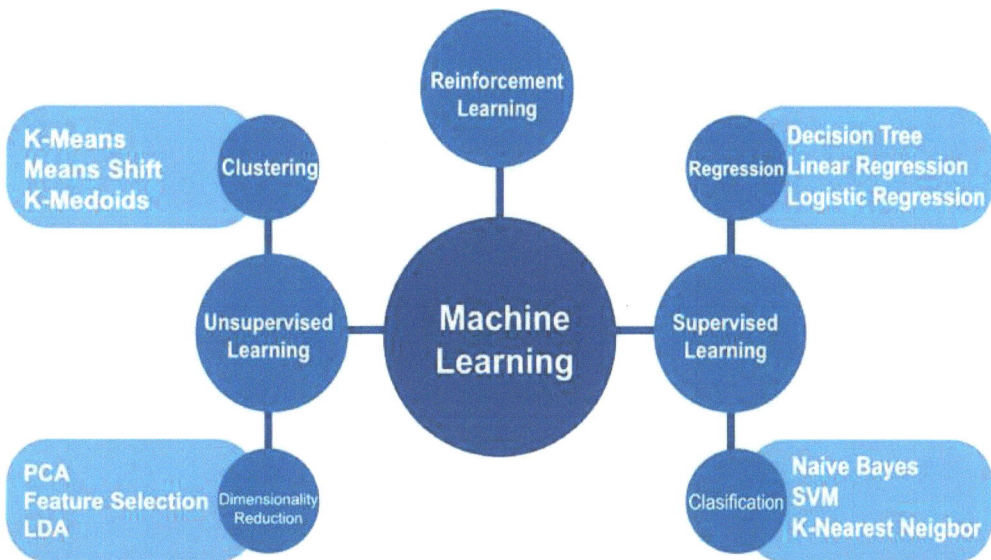

Fig. (3). Generic architecture of machine learning techniques.

In unsupervised learning, targets are not given to models while training, thus models have only input parameters. Without any feedback, it is possible to develop some mechanism that can be used to make decisions and predict future inputs. Dimensionality reduction and clustering are the two simple algorithms in unsupervised learning.

Reinforcement learning is about taking suitable actions to maximize reward in a particular situation. Reinforcement learning differs from supervised learning in a way that in supervised learning the training data has the answer key with it so the model is trained with the correct answer itself whereas in reinforcement learning, there is no answer but the reinforcement agent decides what to do to perform the given task. The combination of physical things, a wide range of networks, IoT, big data, artificial intelligence (AI), Cloud capacity, and process gives rise to smart systems [87].

Sarker stated that various application areas including business intelligence, smart healthcare, smart cities, cybersecurity intelligence, and many more remain the main focus of today's Industry 4.0 due to its technology-driven automation, and smart and intelligent systems. This as a result makes Deep Learning (DL) very crucial today [88]. Its wide range of performance, particularly, its ability to decipher complex architecture in high-dimensional data makes DL technology therefore relevant to artificial intelligence [89] and machine learning [90]. ML and

DL are two AI techniques that are mostly conflated. DL is a subset of ML that essentially uses vast volumes of data and complex algorithms to train a model. Fig. (**4**) illustrates the position of Artificial Intelligence (AI), Machine Learning (ML), and Deep Learning (DL).

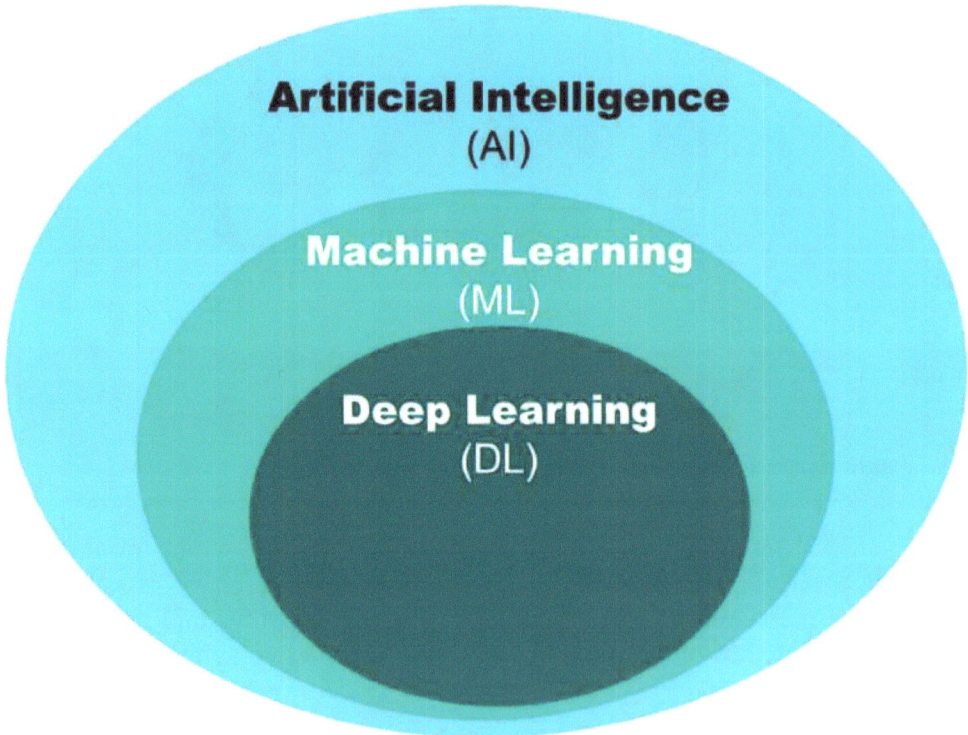

Fig. (4). Illustration of the position of AI, ML, and DL.

Deep Learning technology uses multiple layers to represent the abstractions of data to build computational models. While deep learning takes a long time to train a model due to a large number of parameters, it takes a short amount of time to run during testing as compared to other machine learning algorithms [91].

The three major categories of Deep Learning are; Discriminative learning, Generative learning, and Hybrid Learning. Deep networks for supervised or *discriminative learning* that is utilized to provide a discriminative function in supervised deep learning or classification applications; deep networks for unsupervised or *generative learning* that are used to characterize the high-order correlation properties or features for pattern analysis or synthesis, thus can be used as preprocessing for the supervised algorithm; and deep networks for *hybrid learning* that are an integration of both supervised and unsupervised model and relevant others. We take into account such categories based on the nature and learning capabilities of different DL techniques and how they are used to solve problems in real-world applications [89].

Artificial Intelligence and Machine Learning for SMEs

Artificial intelligence (AI) and/or machine learning (ML) are contemporary technologies that have achieved huge relevance in many sectors, particularly as industry 4.0 drivers such as Google, and as analytics techniques, they are applied to data from IoT devices [68]. Globally, industries are gravitating toward this offshoot of AI and ML approaches, and politicians are attempting to use them to alleviate social problems [92]. Scholars contend that these digital technologies have been effectively employed to create beneficial results in electronic transactions among large corporations to increase performance beyond the control of people, [48], and it has become an essential driver of e-commerce development [93].

In contrast, despite their great contribution to global economic progress, most SMEs in Africa and other developing nations remain adamant and resistant to using these digital tools to reap their related benefits [94, 95]. Additionally, ineptness and underutilization of these digital tools have had a substantial influence on corporate performance, and it is one of the fundamental vulnerabilities in a competitive market. The full potentials of AI and ML for SMEs are yet to be explored and Dwivedi *et al.* attribute this challenge to a lack of education [96]. They emphasize that as much as AI and ML could positively influence productivity and performance, CEOs and managers who lack the absorptive capacity and ability to comprehend these potentials could be a drawback. Horvath and Szabo assessed the slower acceptance rate of AI and ML among SMEs and developing countries and identified the challenge of acceptability and transparency of these digital tools in the business process [68, 97] and also obscurity and disconnection for B2B SMEs, and inadequate financial resources which could be the greatest of all the challenges [6, 67].

SMEs who have effectively used AI and ML in their events can collaborate and interact with their business clients, increase performance, [96, 98] analyze and exploit data, [85, 99], and bring innovativeness and novel approaches in business [96, 100]. Organizations use AI and ML to assess customers' purchase patterns, automate calls and messages, improve advertising, and improve sales [44]. Dwivedi *et al.* add that SMEs have placed AI and ML applications at the heart of automation to execute numerous finance and customer service functions and reconcile payments with invoices, and analyze data to enhance efficiency [101].

These tools involved in analytics, process automation and optimization, dynamic pricing, and prediction contribute to greater revenue generation, increased productivity, dexterity, innovativeness, and better decision-making among SMEs [68, 99, 101]. Many researchers contend that the adoption of AI and ML in e-commerce fastens business processes such as internal operations, better decision-making, new product development, relieving workers for more creative work, and pursuing new markets that ultimately affect business performance which goes beyond human control [93, 102]. With regard to the magnitude of AI/ML adoption, Rahman *et al.* observed that it enhances the link between firms' marketing analytics and capability and holistic marketing decision-making that drives the firms' competitive marketing performance [100]. Basri adds that AI-assisted social media marketing has a significant positive influence on business management and SME performance as well as increased market share and higher revenues [103].

The digitalization race of Industry 4.0 has amplified the requirement for SMEs to clasp digital tools [6]. Entrepreneurs who run and manage SMEs have significant chances and prospects as a result of digitalization to differentiate themselves in the market and expand their enterprises [4]. Most SMEs lack the expertise and capabilities required to capitalize on the most recent digitalization. Nonetheless, international and global corporations gain highly from a combination of cutting-edge digital tools [3, 56]. As a result of this lag, SMEs do not gain as much as big firms gain from the possibilities created by these disruptions. Big organizations, on the other hand, have the advantage of contracting external consultants or IT specialists to use these tools to realize the key drivers of digital transformation that involve the augmentation of business processes, novelty in business models, and customer experience [11, 104, 105].

CONCLUSION

To truly undergo a digital transformation, a company must make fundamental changes to its internal processes, client interactions, and value creation. This all-encompassing shift has far-reaching consequences for an organization, touching on everything from its business model to its culture. It can be said that digital transformation has the potential to unlock important economic values. Yet, there are so many challenges SMEs face in adopting DT. Those challenges include economic/financial, unskilled labour, lack of IT infrastructure, and data security issues.

REFERENCES

[1]   Teece DJ. Business models and dynamic capabilities. Long Range Plann 2018; 51(1): 40-9.
        [http://dx.doi.org/10.1016/j.lrp.2017.06.007]

[2]   Nambisan S, Wright M, Feldman M. The digital transformation of innovation and entrepreneurship: Progress, challenges and key themes. Res Policy 2019; 48(8): 103773.
[http://dx.doi.org/10.1016/j.respol.2019.03.018]

[3]   Aaldering LJ, Song CH. Of leaders and laggards - Towards digitalization of the process industries. Technovation 2021; 105: 102211.
[http://dx.doi.org/10.1016/j.technovation.2020.102211]

[4]   Matarazzo M, Penco L, Profumo G, Quaglia R. Digital transformation and customer value creation in Made in Italy SMEs: A dynamic capabilities perspective. J Bus Res 2021; 123: 642-56.
[http://dx.doi.org/10.1016/j.jbusres.2020.10.033]

[5]   Lorenzo O, Kawalek P, Wharton L. Entrepreneurship, Innovation and Technology: A Guide to Core Models and Tools. 1st ed., Routledge 2018. Available from: https://www.taylorfrancis.com/books/9781351018418
[http://dx.doi.org/10.4324/9781351018425]

[6]   Ghobakhloo M, Iranmanesh M. Digital transformation success under Industry 4.0: A strategic guideline for manufacturing SMEs. J Manuf Tech Manag 2021; 32(8): 1533-56.
[http://dx.doi.org/10.1108/JMTM-11-2020-0455]

[7]   Ardito L, Petruzzelli AM, Panniello U, Garavelli AC. Towards industry 4.0. Bus Process Manag J 2019; 25(2): 323-46.
[http://dx.doi.org/10.1108/BPMJ-04-2017-0088]

[8]   Seyedghorban Z, Tahernejad H, Meriton R, Graham G. Supply chain digitalization: Past, present and future. Prod Plann Contr 2020; 31(2-3): 96-114.
[http://dx.doi.org/10.1080/09537287.2019.1631461]

[9]   Holmström J, Holweg M, Lawson B, Pil FK, Wagner SM. The digitalization of operations and supply chain management: Theoretical and methodological implications. J Oper Manage 2019; 65(8): 728-34.
[http://dx.doi.org/10.1002/joom.1073]

[10]   AlMulhim AF. Smart supply chain and firm performance: The role of digital technologies. Bus Process Manag J 2021; 27(5): 1353-72.
[http://dx.doi.org/10.1108/BPMJ-12-2020-0573]

[11]   Lee KL, Azmi NAN, Hanaysha JR, Alzoubi HM, Alshurideh MT. The effect of digital supply chain on organizational performance. An empirical study in Malaysia manufacturing industry 2022; 10(2): 495-510.

[12]   North K, Aramburu N, Lorenzo OJ. Promoting digitally enabled growth in SMEs: A framework proposal. J Enterp Inf Manag 2019; 33(1): 238-62.
[http://dx.doi.org/10.1108/JEIM-04-2019-0103]

[13]   Quinton S, Canhoto A, Molinillo S, Pera R, Budhathoki T. Conceptualising a digital orientation: Antecedents of supporting SME performance in the digital economy. J Strateg Mark 2018; 26(5): 427-39.
[http://dx.doi.org/10.1080/0965254X.2016.1258004]

[14]   Rahayu R, Day J. E-commerce adoption by SMEs in developing countries: Evidence from Indonesia. Eurasian Business Review 2017; 7(1): 25-41.
[http://dx.doi.org/10.1007/s40821-016-0044-6]

[15]   Tarutė A, Gatautis R. ICT Impact on SMEs Performance. Procedia Soc Behav Sci 2014; 110: 1218-25.
[http://dx.doi.org/10.1016/j.sbspro.2013.12.968]

[16]   Jones P, Simmons G, Packham G, Beynon-Davies P, Pickernell D. An exploration of the attitudes and strategic responses of sole-proprietor micro-enterprises in adopting information and communication technology. Int Small Bus J 2014; 32(3): 285-306.
[http://dx.doi.org/10.1177/0266242612461802]

[17]   Agwu EM, Murray PJ. Empirical study of barriers to electronic commerce uptake by SMEs in developing economies. Int J Innov Digit Econ 2015; 6(2): 1-19.
[http://dx.doi.org/10.4018/ijide.2015040101]

[18]   Napitupulu D, Syafrullah M, Rahim R, Abdullah D, Setiawan MI. Analysis of user readiness toward ICT usage at small medium enterprise in south tangerang. J Phys Conf Ser 2018; 1007: 012042.
[http://dx.doi.org/10.1088/1742-6596/1007/1/012042]

[19]   Keller J, von der Gracht HA. The influence of information and communication technology (ICT) on future foresight processes — Results from a Delphi survey. Technol Forecast Soc Change 2014; 85: 81-92.
[http://dx.doi.org/10.1016/j.techfore.2013.07.010]

[20]   Mazzarol T, Clark DN, Reboud S. Strategy in action: Case studies of strategy, planning and innovation in Australian SMEs. Small Enterp Res 2014; 21(1): 54-71.
[http://dx.doi.org/10.1080/13215906.2014.11082076]

[21]   Dar IA, Mishra M. Dimensional impact of social capital on financial performance of SMEs. J Entrepsh 2020; 29(1): 38-52.
[http://dx.doi.org/10.1177/0971355719893499]

[22]   Odoom R, Agbemabiese GC, Anning-Dorson T, Mensah P. Branding capabilities and SME performance in an emerging market. Mark Intell Plann 2017; 35(4): 473-87.
[http://dx.doi.org/10.1108/MIP-08-2016-0138]

[23]   Tobora OO. Challenges faced by entrepreneurs and the performance of small and medium scale (SMEs) in Nigeria: An intellectual capital issue. International Letters of Social and Humanistic Sciences 2014; 42: 32-40.
[http://dx.doi.org/10.18052/www.scipress.com/ILSHS.42.32]

[24]   Akinyemi F, Adejumo O. Entrepreneurial motives and challenges of SMEs owners in emerging economies: Nigeria & South Africa. aeb 2017; 5(11): 624-33.

[25]   Britzelmaier B, Graue C, Sterk M. Big data in SMEs – findings of an empirical study. Global Business and Economics Review 2020; 22(1/2): 115.
[http://dx.doi.org/10.1504/GBER.2020.105034]

[26]   Tob-Ogu A, Kumar N, Cullen J. ICT adoption in road freight transport in Nigeria – A case study of the petroleum downstream sector. Technol Forecast Soc Change 2018; 131: 240-52.
[http://dx.doi.org/10.1016/j.techfore.2017.09.021]

[27]   Elbeltagi I, Hamad H, Moizer J, Abou-Shouk MA. Levels of business to business e-commerce adoption and competitive advantage in small and medium-sized enterprises: A comparison study between egypt and the united states. J Global Inform Tech Manag 2016; 19(1): 6-25.
[http://dx.doi.org/10.1080/1097198X.2016.1134169]

[28]   Zafar A, Mustafa S. SMEs and its role in economic and socio-economic development of pakistan. International Journal of Academic Research in Accounting, Finance and Management Sciences 2017; 7(4): 195-205.
[http://dx.doi.org/10.6007/IJARAFMS/v7-i4/3484]

[29]   Yunis M, El-Kassar AN, Tarhini A. Impact of ICT-based innovations on organizational performance. J Enterp Inf Manag 2017; 30(1): 122-41.
[http://dx.doi.org/10.1108/JEIM-01-2016-0040]

[30]   Nozari H, Fallah M, Kazemipoor H, Najafi SE. Big data analysis of IoT-based supply chain management considering FMCG industries. Bus Info 2021; 15(1): 78-96.
[http://dx.doi.org/10.17323/2587-814X.2021.1.78.96]

[31]   Holland CP, Thornton SC, Naudé P. B2B analytics in the airline market: Harnessing the power of consumer big data. Ind Mark Manage 2020; 86: 52-64.
[http://dx.doi.org/10.1016/j.indmarman.2019.11.002]

[32] Kazançoğlu Y, Sağnak M, Lafcı Ç, Luthra S, Kumar A, Taçoğlu C. Big data-enabled solutions framework to overcoming the barriers to circular economy initiatives in healthcare sector. Int J Environ Res Public Health 2021; 18(14): 7513.
[http://dx.doi.org/10.3390/ijerph18147513] [PMID: 34299964]

[33] Batko K, Ślęzak A. The use of big data analytics in healthcare. J Big Data 2022; 9(1): 3.
[http://dx.doi.org/10.1186/s40537-021-00553-4] [PMID: 35013701]

[34] Zarezadeh ZZ, Rastegar R, Xiang Z. Big data analytics and hotel guest experience: A critical analysis of the literature. Int J Contemp Hosp Manag 2022; 34(6): 2320-36.
[http://dx.doi.org/10.1108/IJCHM-10-2021-1293]

[35] Fosso Wamba S, Akter S, Edwards A, Chopin G, Gnanzou D. How 'big data' can make big impact: Findings from a systematic review and a longitudinal case study. Int J Prod Econ 2015; 165: 234-46.
[http://dx.doi.org/10.1016/j.ijpe.2014.12.031]

[36] Ruggles S, Fitch CA, Roberts E. Historical census record linkage. Annu Rev Sociol 2018; 44(1): 19-37.
[http://dx.doi.org/10.1146/annurev-soc-073117-041447] [PMID: 30369709]

[37] Kaufmann M. Big data management canvas: A reference model for value creation from data. Big Data and Cognitive Computing 2019; 3(1): 19.
[http://dx.doi.org/10.3390/bdcc3010019]

[38] Mikalef P, Boura M, Lekakos G, Krogstie J. Big data analytics and firm performance: Findings from a mixed-method approach. J Bus Res 2019; 98: 261-76.
[http://dx.doi.org/10.1016/j.jbusres.2019.01.044]

[39] Rialti R, Marzi G, Caputo A, Mayah KA. Achieving strategic flexibility in the era of big data. Manage Decis 2020; 58(8): 1585-600.
[http://dx.doi.org/10.1108/MD-09-2019-1237]

[40] Olabode OE, Boso N, Hultman M, Leonidou CN. Big data analytics capability and market performance: The roles of disruptive business models and competitive intensity. J Bus Res 2022; 139: 1218-30.
[http://dx.doi.org/10.1016/j.jbusres.2021.10.042]

[41] Gupta V, Singh VK, Ghose U, Mukhija P. A quantitative and text-based characterization of big data research. In: Pinto D, Singh V, Eds. IFS. 2019; 36: pp. (5)4659-575.
[http://dx.doi.org/10.3233/JIFS-179016]

[42] Mariani M, Baggio R. Big data and analytics in hospitality and tourism: A systematic literature review. Int J Contemp Hosp Manag 2022; 34(1): 231-78.
[http://dx.doi.org/10.1108/IJCHM-03-2021-0301]

[43] Fosso Wamba S, Kala Kamdjoug JR, Epie Bawack R, Keogh JG. Bitcoin, Blockchain and Fintech: A systematic review and case studies in the supply chain. Prod Plann Contr 2020; 31(2-3): 115-42.
[http://dx.doi.org/10.1080/09537287.2019.1631460]

[44] Benzidia S, Makaoui N, Bentahar O. The impact of big data analytics and artificial intelligence on green supply chain process integration and hospital environmental performance. Technol Forecast Soc Change 2021; 165: 120557.
[http://dx.doi.org/10.1016/j.techfore.2020.120557]

[45] Philip Chen CL, Zhang CY. Data-intensive applications, challenges, techniques and technologies: A survey on Big Data. Inf Sci 2014; 275: 314-47.
[http://dx.doi.org/10.1016/j.ins.2014.01.015]

[46] Gandomi A, Haider M. Beyond the hype: Big data concepts, methods, and analytics. Int J Inf Manage 2015; 35(2): 137-44.
[http://dx.doi.org/10.1016/j.ijinfomgt.2014.10.007]

[47] Hazen BT, Boone CA, Ezell JD, Jones-Farmer LA. Data quality for data science, predictive analytics, and big data in supply chain management: An introduction to the problem and suggestions for research and applications. Int J Prod Econ 2014; 154: 72-80.
[http://dx.doi.org/10.1016/j.ijpe.2014.04.018]

[48] Agrawal D. Philip Bernstein, Elisa Bertino, Davidson S, Umeshwas Dayal. Challenges and Opportunities with Big Data 2011.

[49] Moktadir MA, Ali SM, Paul SK, Shukla N. Barriers to big data analytics in manufacturing supply chains: A case study from Bangladesh. Comput Ind Eng 2019; 128: 1063-75.
[http://dx.doi.org/10.1016/j.cie.2018.04.013]

[50] Bertello A, Ferraris A, Bresciani S, De Bernardi P. Big data analytics (BDA) and degree of internationalization: The interplay between governance of BDA infrastructure and BDA capabilities. J Manag Gov 2021; 25(4): 1035-55.
[http://dx.doi.org/10.1007/s10997-020-09542-w]

[51] Coleman S, Göb R, Manco G, Pievatolo A, Tort-Martorell X, Reis MS. How Can SMEs Benefit from Big Data? Challenges and a path forward. Qual Reliab Eng Int 2016; 32(6): 2151-64.
[http://dx.doi.org/10.1002/qre.2008]

[52] Verma S, Bhattacharyya SS, Kumar S. An extension of the technology acceptance model in the big data analytics system implementation environment. Inf Process Manage 2018; 54(5): 791-806.
[http://dx.doi.org/10.1016/j.ipm.2018.01.004]

[53] Wang L, Yang M, Pathan ZH, Salam S, Shahzad K, Zeng J. Analysis of influencing factors of big data adoption in chinese enterprises using DANP technique. Sustainability 2018; 10(11): 3956.
[http://dx.doi.org/10.3390/su10113956]

[54] Mathias Kalema B, Mokgadi M. Developing countries organizations' readiness for Big Data analytics. Probl Perspect Manag 2017; 15(1): 260-70.
[http://dx.doi.org/10.21511/ppm.15(1-1).2017.13]

[55] Malaka I, Brown I. Challenges to the organisational adoption of big data analytics: A case study in the south african telecommunications industry. Proceedings of the 2015 Annual Research Conference on South African Institute of Computer Scientists and Information Technologists - SAICSIT '15. Stellenbosch, South Africa: ACM Press 2015; pp. 1-9.http://dl.acm.org/citation.cfm?doid=2815782.2815793 Internet
[http://dx.doi.org/10.1145/2815782.2815793]

[56] Parra-Sánchez DT, Talero-Sarmiento LH, Guerrero CD. Assessment of ICT policies for digital transformation in Colombia: technology readiness for IoT adoption in SMEs in the trading sector. Digital Policy, Regulation and Governance 2021; 23(4): 412-31.
[http://dx.doi.org/10.1108/DPRG-09-2020-0120]

[57] Big iot data analytics: Architecture, opportunities, and open research challenges. IEEE Access 2017; 5: 5247-61.
[http://dx.doi.org/10.1109/ACCESS.2017.2689040]

[58] Kaur J, Kaur K. Guru Nanak Dev University/Department of CET. Internet of Things: A Review on Technologies, Architecture, Challenges, Applications, Future Trends. International Journal of Computer Network and Information Security 2017; 9(4): 57-70.
[http://dx.doi.org/10.5815/ijcnis.2017.04.07]

[59] Mahmoud R, Yousuf T, Aloul F, Zualkernan I. Internet of things (IoT) security: Current status, challenges and prospective measures In: 2015 10th International Conference for Internet Technology and Secured Transactions (ICITST). London, United Kingdom: IEEE 2015; pp. 336-41.http://ieeexplore.ieee.org/document/7412116/ Internet

[60] Santos L, Rabadao C, Goncalves R. Intrusion detection systems in Internet of Things: A literature review In: 2018 13th Iberian Conference on Information Systems and Technologies (CISTI). Caceres:

IEEE 2018; pp. 1-7.https://ieeexplore.ieee.org/document/8399291/ Internet

[61]   Heady R, Luger G, Maccabe A, Servilla M. Heady R, Luger G, Maccabe A, Servilla M. The architecture of a network level intrusion detection system. 1990. Available from: http://www.osti.gov/servlets/purl/425295-4IN2Pw/webviewable/ (Accessed on 2022 Nov 19).

[62]   Dali L, Mivule K, El-Sayed H. A heuristic attack detection approach using the "least weighted" attributes for cyber security data In: 2017 Intelligent Systems Conference (IntelliSys). London: IEEE 2017; pp. 1067-73.http://ieeexplore.ieee.org/document/8324260/ Internet [http://dx.doi.org/10.1109/IntelliSys.2017.8324260]

[63]   Shifa A, Asghar MN, Fleury M. Multimedia security perspectives in IoT In: 2016 sixth international conference on innovative computing technology (INTECH). Dublin, Ireland: IEEE 2016; pp. 550-5.http://ieeexplore.ieee.org/document/7845081/ Internet [http://dx.doi.org/10.1109/INTECH.2016.7845081]

[64]   Abazi B. An approach to the impact of transformation from the traditional use of ICT to the Internet of Things: How smart solutions can transform SMEs. IFAC-PapersOnLine 2016; 49(29): 148-51. [http://dx.doi.org/10.1016/j.ifacol.2016.11.091]

[65]   Carcary M, Maccani G, Doherty E, Conway G. Exploring the determinants of iot adoption: Findings from a systematic literature review. In: Zdravkovic J, Grabis J, Nurcan S, Stirna J, Eds. Perspectives in Business Informatics Research. Cham: Springer International Publishing 2018; pp. 113-25.http://link.springer.com/10.1007/978-3-319-99951-7_8

[66]   Shin DI. An exploratory study of innovation strategies of the internet of things SMEs in South Korea. Asia Pacific Journal of Innovation and Entrepreneurship 2017; 11(2): 171-89. [http://dx.doi.org/10.1108/APJIE-08-2017-025]

[67]   Masood T, Sonntag P. Industry 4.0: Adoption challenges and benefits for SMEs. Comput Ind 2020; 121: 103261. [http://dx.doi.org/10.1016/j.compind.2020.103261]

[68]   Hansen EB, Bøgh S. Artificial intelligence and internet of things in small and medium-sized enterprises: A survey. J Manuf Syst 2021; 58: 362-72. [http://dx.doi.org/10.1016/j.jmsy.2020.08.009]

[69]   Neagu G, Ianculescu M, Alexandru A, Florian V, Rădulescu CZ. Next generation IoT and its influence on decision-making. An illustrative case study. Procedia Comput Sci 2019; 162: 555-61. [http://dx.doi.org/10.1016/j.procs.2019.12.023]

[70]   Consoli D. Literature analysis on determinant factors and the impact of ICT in SMEs. Procedia Soc Behav Sci 2012; 62: 93-7. [http://dx.doi.org/10.1016/j.sbspro.2012.09.016]

[71]   Awa HO, Ojiabo OU, Emecheta BC. Integrating TAM, TPB and TOE frameworks and expanding their characteristic constructs for e-commerce adoption by SMEs. Journal of Science & Technology Policy Management 2015; 6(1): 76-94. [http://dx.doi.org/10.1108/JSTPM-04-2014-0012]

[72]   Fathian M, Akhavan P, Hoorali M. E-readiness assessment of non-profit ICT SMEs in a developing country: The case of Iran. Technovation 2008; 28(9): 578-90. [http://dx.doi.org/10.1016/j.technovation.2008.02.002]

[73]   Giotopoulos I, Kontolaimou A, Korra E, Tsakanikas A. What drives ICT adoption by SMEs? Evidence from a large-scale survey in Greece. J Bus Res 2017; 81: 60-9. [http://dx.doi.org/10.1016/j.jbusres.2017.08.007]

[74]   Adane M. Cloud computing adoption: Strategies for Sub-Saharan Africa SMEs for enhancing competitiveness. Afr J Sci Technol Innov Dev 2018; 10(2): 197-207. [http://dx.doi.org/10.1080/20421338.2018.1439288]

[75]   Hoque MR, Saif ANM, AlBar AM, Bao Y. Adoption of information and communication technology

for development. Inf Dev 2016; 32(4): 986-1000.
[http://dx.doi.org/10.1177/0266666915578202]

[76]   Eze SC, Awa HO, Okoye JC, Emecheta BC, Anazodo RO. Determinant factors of information communication technology *(ICT)* adoption by government□owned universities in Nigeria. J Enterp Inf Manag 2013; 26(4): 427-43.
[http://dx.doi.org/10.1108/JEIM-05-2013-0024]

[77]   Kannabiran G, Dharmalingam P. Enablers and inhibitors of advanced information technologies adoption by SMEs. J Enterp Inf Manag 2012; 25(2): 186-209.
[http://dx.doi.org/10.1108/17410391211204419]

[78]   Nylander S, Wallberg A, Hansson P. Challenges for SMEs entering the IoT world: success is about so much more than technology.Proceedings of the Seventh International Conference on the Internet of Things. Linz, Austria: ACM 2017; pp. 1-7.https://dl.acm.org/doi/10.1145/3131542.3131547 Internet
[http://dx.doi.org/10.1145/3131542.3131547]

[79]   Zhao X, Zhang L. Discussion on the development of E-business pattern in Internet of Things environment In: 2013 chinese automation congress. Changsha, Hunan, China: IEEE 2013; pp. 918-23.http://ieeexplore.ieee.org/document/6775863/ Internet
[http://dx.doi.org/10.1109/CAC.2013.6775863]

[80]   Forsstrom S, Jennehag U, Guan X. A plain low threshold iot platform for enabling new iot products from SMEs In: 2020 IEEE international workshop on metrology for industry 40 & IoT. Roma, Italy: IEEE 2020; pp. 390-4.https://ieeexplore.ieee.org/document/9138303/ Internet
[http://dx.doi.org/10.1109/MetroInd4.0IoT48571.2020.9138303]

[81]   Vermanen M, Rantanen MM, Harkke V. Ethical framework for IoT deployment in SMEs: Individual perspective. Internet Res 2022; 32(7): 185-201.
[http://dx.doi.org/10.1108/INTR-08-2019-0361]

[82]   Leminen S, Rajahonka M, Westerlund M, Wendelin R. The future of the internet of things: toward heterarchical ecosystems and service business models. J Bus Ind Mark 2018; 33(6): 749-67.
[http://dx.doi.org/10.1108/JBIM-10-2015-0206]

[83]   Bauernhansl T, ten Hompel M, Vogel-Heuser B, Eds. Industrie 40 in Produktion, Automatisierung und Logistik. Wiesbaden: Springer Fachmedien Wiesbaden 2014.http://link.springer.com/10.1007/978-3-658-04682-8 Internet
[http://dx.doi.org/10.1007/978-3-658-04682-8]

[84]   Gubbi J, Buyya R, Marusic S, Palaniswami M. Internet of Things (IoT): A vision, architectural elements, and future directions. Future Gener Comput Syst 2013; 29(7): 1645-60.
[http://dx.doi.org/10.1016/j.future.2013.01.010]

[85]   Alter S. Understanding artificial intelligence in the context of usage: Contributions and smartness of algorithmic capabilities in work systems. Int J Inf Manage 2022; 67: 102392.
[http://dx.doi.org/10.1016/j.ijinfomgt.2021.102392]

[86]   Syam N, Sharma A. Waiting for a sales renaissance in the fourth industrial revolution: Machine learning and artificial intelligence in sales research and practice. Ind Mark Manage 2018; 69: 135-46.
[http://dx.doi.org/10.1016/j.indmarman.2017.12.019]

[87]   Aheleroff S, Xu X, Lu Y, *et al.* IoT-enabled smart appliances under industry 4.0: A case study. Adv Eng Inform 2020; 43: 101043.
[http://dx.doi.org/10.1016/j.aei.2020.101043]

[88]   Sarker IH. Data science and analytics: An overview from data-driven smart computing, decision-making and applications perspective. SN Computer Science 2021; 2(5): 377.
[http://dx.doi.org/10.1007/s42979-021-00765-8] [PMID: 34278328]

[89]   Sarker IH, Furhad MH, Nowrozy R. AI-driven cybersecurity: An overview, security intelligence modeling and research directions. SN Computer Science 2021; 2(3): 173.

[http://dx.doi.org/10.1007/s42979-021-00557-0] [PMID: 33778771]

[90]   Sarker IH. Machine Learning: Algorithms, real-world applications and research directions. SN Computer Science 2021; 2(3): 160.
[http://dx.doi.org/10.1007/s42979-021-00592-x] [PMID: 33778771]

[91]   Xin Y, Kong L, Liu Z, *et al.* Machine learning and deep learning methods for cybersecurity. IEEE Access 2018; 6: 35365-81.
[http://dx.doi.org/10.1109/ACCESS.2018.2836950]

[92]   Prem E. Artificial intelligence for innovation in austria. Technol Innov Manag Rev 2019; 9(12): 5-15.
[http://dx.doi.org/10.22215/timreview/1287]

[93]   Song X, Yang S, Huang Z, Huang T. The application of artificial intelligence in electronic commerce. J Phys Conf Ser 2019; 1302(3): 032030.
[http://dx.doi.org/10.1088/1742-6596/1302/3/032030]

[94]   Abed SS. Social commerce adoption using TOE framework: An empirical investigation of Saudi Arabian SMEs. Int J Inf Manage 2020; 53: 102118.
[http://dx.doi.org/10.1016/j.ijinfomgt.2020.102118]

[95]   i M, Sm S. A study of the effectiveness of e-commerce adoption among small and medium-sized enterprise (SME) in postnatal care services industry: a case study in selangor, malaysia. Int J Psychosoc Rehabil 2020; 24(1): 779-83.
[http://dx.doi.org/10.37200/IJPR/V24I1/PR200182]

[96]   Dwivedi YK, Hughes L, Ismagilova E, *et al.* Artificial Intelligence (AI): Multidisciplinary perspectives on emerging challenges, opportunities, and agenda for research, practice and policy. Int J Inf Manage 2021; 57: 101994.
[http://dx.doi.org/10.1016/j.ijinfomgt.2019.08.002]

[97]   Horváth D, Szabó RZ. Driving forces and barriers of Industry 4.0: Do multinational and small and medium-sized companies have equal opportunities? Technol Forecast Soc Change 2019; 146: 119-32.
[http://dx.doi.org/10.1016/j.techfore.2019.05.021]

[98]   Brink T. B2B SME management of antecedents to the application of social media. Ind Mark Manage 2017; 64: 57-65.
[http://dx.doi.org/10.1016/j.indmarman.2017.02.007]

[99]   Akter S, McCarthy G, Sajib S, *et al.* Algorithmic bias in data-driven innovation in the age of AI. Int J Inf Manage 2021; 60: 102387.
[http://dx.doi.org/10.1016/j.ijinfomgt.2021.102387]

[100]   Rahman MS, Hossain MA, Abdel Fattah FAM. Does marketing analytics capability boost firms' competitive marketing performance in data-rich business environment? J Enterp Inf Manag 2022; 35(2): 455-80.
[http://dx.doi.org/10.1108/JEIM-05-2020-0185]

[101]   Dwivedi YK, Hughes L, Ismagilova E, *et al.* Artificial Intelligence (AI): Multidisciplinary perspectives on emerging challenges, opportunities, and agenda for research, practice and policy. Int J Inf Manage 2021; 57: 101994.
[http://dx.doi.org/10.1016/j.ijinfomgt.2019.08.002]

[102]   Zhang D, Pee LG, Cui L. Artificial intelligence in E-commerce fulfillment: A case study of resource orchestration at Alibaba's Smart Warehouse. Int J Inf Manage 2021; 57: 102304.
[http://dx.doi.org/10.1016/j.ijinfomgt.2020.102304]

[103]   Basri W. Examining the impact of artificial intelligence (AI)-. Assisted Social Media Marketing on the Performance of Small and Medium Enterprises: Toward Effective Business Management in the Saudi Arabian Context: IJCIS 2020; 13(1): 142.

[104]   Chatterjee S, Rana NP, Dwivedi YK, Baabdullah AM. Understanding AI adoption in manufacturing and production firms using an integrated TAM-TOE model. Technol Forecast Soc Change 2021; 170:

120880.
[http://dx.doi.org/10.1016/j.techfore.2021.120880]

[105] Ferraris A, Giachino C, Ciampi F, Couturier J. R&D internationalization in medium-sized firms: The moderating role of knowledge management in enhancing innovation performances. J Bus Res 2021; 128: 711-8.
[http://dx.doi.org/10.1016/j.jbusres.2019.11.003]

CHAPTER 2

Factors Influencing the Adoption of Online Shopping and Its Influence on Consumers' Intention to Shop Online: A Study of SMEs in Ghana

Mohammed Majeed[1,*], Asare Charles[2], Yomboi Jonas[3], Nana Arko-Cole[4] and Ahmed Tijani[5]

[1] *Department of Marketing, Tamale Technical University, Tamale-Ghana*

[2] *Ghana Communication Technology University, Tamale, Northern Region, Ghana*

[3] *University for Developing Studies, Tamale, Northern Region, Ghana*

[4] *University of Professional Studies, Accra, Tamale, Northern Region, Ghana*

[5] *Minerals Commission, Tamale, Northern Region, Ghana*

Abstract: The commercial landscape has been transformed by globalization and the rise of technological innovation. Many firms are now using information technology when it comes to providing services to their clients. To that end, a survey of consumers of online products in Ghana was conducted to learn more about the variables that drive the uptake of online shopping and how that affects customers' willingness to do so. This study employed a quantitative approach to investigate the association between characteristics that encourage online purchasing and online shopping intentions. The independent variables employed in the research were simplicity of use, usefulness, risk, and convenience. Research indicated that describing online purchasing as easy, beneficial, risk-free, and convenient had a substantial positive impact on consumer online purchase intention. That is why internet purchasing and its determinants were shown to be directly linked and of substantial importance.

Keywords: Adoption, Consumer behaviour, Online, Shopping, SMEs.

INTRODUCTION

Human requirements can no longer be met without innovation. Thus, innovation is imperative in order to reach long-term objectives due to globalization, fast technology improvement, and a rise in online customer expectations [1]. E-com-

[*] **Corresponding author Mohammed Majeed:** Department of Marketing, Tamale Technical University, Tamale-Ghana; E-mail: tunteya14june@gmail.com

Mohammed Majeed, Abdul-Razak Abubakari, Awini Gideon and Jayadatta S. (Eds.)

merce enables customers to acquire access rapidly and easily to data as well as information, skills, and knowledge [2]. E-commerce has the potential to improve the competitiveness of emerging nations while also alleviating poverty [2].

According to Isohella *et al.* [3], the arrival of internet technology in our daily lives and routines has had a positive influence on our lives and companies throughout the globe [4]. As a result of the Internet, companies and people alike have been able to interact and receive information in a variety of new ways that were previously unavailable [5]. One of the most crucial components of modern-day information technology is e-commerce, or the buying and selling of goods and services through the Internet [6, 7]. It seems, on the surface, that internet commerce is fast becoming a successful technique of doing business in almost every corner of the globe [8]. This has encouraged consumers to shift their purchasing habits in favor of the Internet shopping. The result is an increase in the number of e-commerce websites offering great deals and discounts to entice customers to buy their needs, particularly in the retail sector [9].

It has been observed that the reaction to online shopping has expanded swiftly in many regions of the globe, regardless of the many factors that determine its adoption in every place [10]. Compared to other African nations, the internet penetration of Ghanaian consumers is quite high. When it comes to their marketing efforts, more and more Ghanaians are turning to internet shopping as a whole new kind of trade [7]. Ghana has the second-fastest smartphone market penetration in Africa, according to a prior survey [11]. Though it is still in its infancy in lower-middle-income nations, the online buying system should be taken into account due to its complexity.

This phenomenon of online shopping can only be fully appreciated if one has a thorough understanding of the elements that influence consumers' online purchasing decisions [12]. There are still places in Ghana where internet shopping does not exist, despite the country's growing use of the internet and acceptance of new technologies. Customers' desire to use the Internet as a means of acquiring goods and services is a major concern in this respect. Online purchasing has been extensively studied in wealthy countries, but little research has been done in underdeveloped countries [13]. Studies on information technology (IT) are few in poor nations, resulting in a lack of effective IT adoption [14]. Research demonstrating the acceptability and expansion of online shopping in developing nations is also weak, with the majority of the data relying on personal experience [15]. There is an urgent need to better understand the issue of consumers' opinions and attitudes in market research in order to fill in the information gaps.

We want to obtain a better understanding of the special needs of developing countries like Ghana and how to promote online shopping adoption in these countries, *via* this study.

This we believe will aid SMEs to better forecast and assess online purchase intentions and future advancements in the research field by better-knowing customers' online purchasing behaviour [16]. This article's focus is on Ghanaian customers. We looked at the factors that impact their decision-making process while making an online purchase. As a result, the TAM framework for the present research incorporates participants' perceptions of risk and convenience.

When consumers do not acquire enough information from a website, they tend to hunt for perceived danger. Increasing the likelihood of online shopping may be achieved by lowering shoppers' perceptions of risk [17] and increasing their willingness to take that risk [18]. Return policies are becoming a key instrument for increasing sales and customer loyalty as more and more people begin to use e-commerce for their purchases [19]. Only a small number of academics have looked at how return policies at online stores affect customer behavior [20, 21].

MAIN OBJECTIVE

The main objective of this quantitative correlation research was to investigate the factors responsible for consumers' willingness to adopt online shopping amongst SMEs in Ghana.

Specific Objectives

1. To establish whether online perceived ease of use has a significant positive influence on online shopping intention amongst consumers of SMEs in Ghana.

2. To find out whether online perceived usefulness has a significant positive influence on online shopping intention amongst the consumers of SMEs in Ghana.

3. To determine whether online perceived convenience has a significant positive influence on online shopping intention amongst consumers of SMEs in Ghana.

4. To find out whether the online perceived risk has a significant positive influence on online shopping intention amongst consumers of SMEs in Ghana.

SIGNIFICANCE OF THE STUDY

For small and medium-sized enterprises (SMEs) operating in Ghana, knowledge, and skills in successful e-commerce, adoption methods are critical. In order to boost competitiveness, customer base, and market share, the study's results would be shared with Ghana's small and medium-sized enterprise (SME) owners. Adopting e-commerce may help SMEs grow their consumer base and increase their supply chain's efficiency [22]. Ghanaian SMEs might utilize the study's findings to improve their internet platforms and retail operations both at home and abroad [23, 24].

There might be strong evidence that there is a statistically significant correlation between the PU of e-commerce platforms and the desire to embrace online purchasing, which could lead to the successful adoption of e-commerce platforms in order to expand enterprises. The lack of a statistically significant correlation indicates that researchers should look at other factors that may impact customer desire to use Internet purchasing. Ghanaian SMEs may be able to better grasp crucial factors that impact customers' choices to use internet purchasing as a good social change. Business executives may benefit from this insight, which might lead to a reduction in unemployment in the online retail sector. Having fewer people out of work might have a positive impact on the lives of both prospective workers and customers.

LITERATURE REVIEW

Small and Medium Enterprises

Small and medium-sized enterprises (SMEs) play a crucial role in every developed economy. Many experts in the field of economics believe that a country's economy thrives on the strength of its many different types of small and medium-sized businesses (SMEs) [25]. Growth, new employment opportunities, new products and services, and tax income are all propelled by the success of the nation's small and medium-sized companies (SMEs) [26]. It has been shown that SMEs play an important role in creating and strengthening economies by providing employment opportunities, fostering the accumulation of personal wealth, combating poverty, and bringing in tax money [27, 28]. Aga, Francis, and Rodriguez Meza [29] emphasized the prevalence of SMEs that contribute to the battle against global poverty by driving economic development, providing employment opportunities, and reducing poverty overall.

Experts in labour market data often point to SMBs as the private sector's main employer [29]. Katua [30] found that the degree to which a country's citizens suffer poverty, unemployment, economic success, and good quality of living was connected with the health of its small and medium-sized companies (SMEs). Those responsible for running small and medium-sized businesses (SMEs) in Ghana are crucial in the country's economic growth. Growth of the labour force is a key indicator of a country's ability to support small and medium-sized enterprises (SMEs). Ayyagari, Demirguc Kunt, and Maksimovic [31] examined cross-sectional data from 104 countries to conclude that small and medium-sized enterprises (SMEs) are responsible for creating new employment. Research by Ndiaye, N., Razak, L. A., Nagayev, R., and Ng., A. (2018), found that SMEs accounted for more than 60% of total employment in developing nations. In addition, SMEs are responsible for 40% of the increase in developing nations' GDP in 2018. In Ghana, SMEs make up over 85% of the private sector and contribute around 70% of GDP (International Trade Centre, 2016) [32]. According to data compiled by Ghana's Registrar General's Office, 90% of the country's enterprises are classified as SMEs [33]. Ghana's economic progress may be attributed, in large part, to the efforts of its small and medium-sized firms (SMEs).

According to research by Quartey, Turkson, Abor, and Iddrisu [34], e-commerce has the potential to improve the marketing efforts of small and medium-sized enterprises (SMEs). However, it is known that it may be difficult for small and medium-sized firms to get financing from banks and other lending organisations (SMEs). Businesses in over 120 countries were polled using data from the World Bank Enterprise Survey, and the findings showed that SMEs had a hard time securing bank loans. "There is a belief that most loan officers lack a strong grasp of small business cycles and are hesitant to lend to SMEs in general," [35].

According to Fiseha and Oyelana (2015), there are a number of difficulties that SMEs in developing countries must overcome. It may be difficult for small and medium-sized businesses (SMEs) to acquire and use cutting-edge technology. In certain countries, human labour is more valuable than any other technological resource. Pierre and Fernandez [36] state that in order to succeed, the leaders of small and medium-sized enterprises (SMEs) are always on the lookout for new ways to allocate their limited human, financial, and technological resources.

Factors for Online Shopping Adoption

Usefulness

Davis [37] argued that the technology's usability and utility play a major role in attracting and retaining online customers. Osama *et al.* [38] define perceived usefulness as "the extent to which an individual believes that adopting a given system will result in the realisation of anticipated advantages". Furthermore, online shoppers' preferences on whether to stick with online shopping or return to more conventional methods may be influenced by their impressions of the usefulness of various apps and tools available to them while doing so. Davis underlined the significance of a person's desire to employ new technology being influenced by their perception of its utility [39]. Perceived utility relates to the extent to which a person thinks online transactions will help him or her increase productivity [40]. There is a lot of evidence that perceived utility has a major impact on e-commerce intention [41 - 44]. Contrary to what most people think, Chen and Mei's [45] study of how college students view and evaluate mobile internet advertising showed that perceived utility does not affect actual usage.

According to IS literature, a system's perceived utility rises in direct proportion to its perceived usefulness [46]. In addition to the work of these individuals, additional scholars have asserted the same (see, for instance, [47-54]). Another study indicated that perceived usefulness did not affect how valuable a product was considered [49]. Hanjaya, Kenny, and Gunawan (2019) say that fail to provide personalized content, customers are more likely to shop somewhere else.

Ease of Use

Perceived ease of use, as defined by Davis [37], refers to the extent to which a user believes that engaging with a system will need less work on their part or will require no effort at all. While it is undeniable that there are many benefits to doing business online, some consumers may be turned off by the need of using interactive websites or applications. However, if the disadvantages of online shopping are minimized to the point where they are outweighed by the benefits, then more people will start making purchases over the internet and fewer people would turn to more conventional means of purchasing goods. There are several variables that might affect sales of an electronic or digital product or service.

Convenience

Furthermore, the convenience associated with online searches pertains to the effortless accessibility of product information on the internet. It is frequently considered a pivotal factor when deciding between online and offline shopping [7, 55]. Customers have a great preference for online distribution channels owing to the high degree of ease that these channels provide. Without requiring a substantial amount of movement, online platforms make available useful information about recently introduced deals, price reductions, and individualized suggestions [56]. Customers may shop for an almost infinite variety of things from many different websites, without being constrained by either time or geography.

When compared to traditional buying, shopping online is characterized by several distinct advantages, the most notable of which is its convenience, which has been cited as the primary reason customers choose to make their purchases online [7]. According to the findings of research carried out by Tarhini *et al.* [57], those who shop for products online are more likely to be seeking convenience. In a manner that is analogous, the study that was conducted by Omotayo and Omotope [7] demonstrates that consumers who choose to make their purchases from online businesses care more about convenience and less about experience. When it comes to deciding whether or not to make a purchase of anything online, these shoppers believe that the ease of the transaction is the single most essential consideration.

Perceived Risk

Perceived risk is "an evaluation of ambiguity or a lack of information on the occurrence of possible outcomes," and it also considers the fact that "one cannot affect the result," according to several definitions from March 1978 [58]. Perceived risk is considered to be an important term in consumer behavior, and it is most frequently utilized to describe both the consumer perceptions of risks as well as the risk reduction measures that customers choose to apply [59]. Cited by Hubert *et al.* [60], King and He (2006) are the ones who first introduced the concept of "perceived risk." They defined it as the "subjective anticipation of incurring a loss in proportion to the anticipated result." This is how the phrase "perceived risk" came to be. The second explanation of this phrase describes it as the degree to which a person retains apprehension about a particular product or service [61]. According to Li and Zhang (2002) [62], the level of perceived risk is made up of two primary components, and both components play a part in the process of influencing the behavior of customers when they are engaged in the activity of online shopping. The first section discusses problems that are associated with financial risk, product risk, and time risk. The second section discusses online transactions and addresses concerns regarding confidentiality and safety.

Students in Ghana make a majority of their purchases from online shopping using mobile money as a form of payment; hence, there is not a broad emphasis on e-transaction security and privacy among students. Students, on the other hand, weigh the pros and drawbacks of in-store *vs.* online shopping in terms of the potential for financial, product, and time loss. Due to the fact that students are able to save time and energy by shopping from the convenience of their halls and hostels, it is clear that navigating the pages of an online shopping site poses no threat to them. According to the findings of research conducted by Wu and Wang [63], there seems to be a strikingly positive and substantial association between the perceived risk and the intention of mobile commerce drivers.

Online Shopping Intention

Purchase intention metrics have seen a lot of usage as a tool for determining the possibility of consumers purchasing things within certain time frames [64]. The consumer's favourable attitude regarding online purchasing has a beneficial impact on the consumer's purchase intention in the beginning. In addition, the consumer's desire to purchase will have a role in the consumer's ultimate purchasing choice as well as the consumer's actual buying behaviour. In addition to this, the research demonstrates that online shopping intentions and overall consumer happiness are intertwined and impact one another. The intents of customers may generally be broken down into three categories: the intention to make a purchase, the desire to increase the amount of time they spend at the online shop, and the intention to suggest the online business to other people [65]. Lesakova's model of online pre-buy intents found that there was a link between shoppers' propensity to go online in search of product details and their propensity to make a purchase on the same platform [66]. Differences in online shopping intentions might be attributed in large part to differences in internet-searching intentions. People who claim they will look for a thing are more likely to purchase those goods than people who indicate they will not look [67]. Furthermore, shoppers online often do further research about a product before making a final purchase [67]. Kim and Park, (2005) discovered that consumers who are interested in learning more about a product are also likely to be interested in making a purchase *via* online channels. Therefore, it is crucial to consider how one finds and receives information while making a buying decision.

Overview of E-commerce in Ghana

In Ghana, the use of e-commerce in the commercial sector is becoming more common. Internet use skyrocketed in Ghana once the country's telecom industry was allowed to become more competitive in the 1990s [68]. The International Telecommunication Union/UNCTAD Digital Opportunity Index investigated the progression of digitalization in Ghana throughout the course of time and compared it to the progression of digitalization in other African nations. This demonstrated a pattern of progress that demonstrates that the level of e-commerce activity in the nation is continuing to improve [65]. Both the industry of information and communications technology and the applications that make use of it have a significant impact on the development of the economies of all nations [69]. The expansion of information and communication technologies, together with the continued use of such technologies by several enterprises, contributes to increased economic growth by diversifying the procedures involved in both domestic and global commerce [69]. The commercial world has realized that, in order to hasten the process, it is necessary to get an understanding of the major aspects that influence the rate at which small and medium-sized enterprises (SMEs) in Ghana use e-commerce technology. Despite the progress made in the field of information and communications technology (ICT), the growth of the information technology business in Ghana has been limited by several obstacles, which have also prevented IT systems from being implemented in key economic sectors [35]. Owners of businesses classified as SMEs must have an understanding of the limitations that have hampered the implementation of information technology systems in essential economic sectors. Access to the internet is an essential component in the dissemination of new technologies. The low number of people with internet access and high-speed broadband connections was a major obstacle for many enterprises in Ghana at the start of Ghana's ICT-led boom in 2005. That is to say, not enough people had access to the internet [35]. One study found that just 1.8% of Ghanaians utilize the internet, well below the regional and global averages of 2.8% and 7.8%, respectively. Currently, over 37.88% of the population of Ghana is online. This is much higher than the average of 24.48% in the African region but lower than the average of 45.58% among developing countries [70]. It is necessary for small and medium-sized company owners to have access to Internet services in order to be able to utilize e-commerce as a means of marketing their goods.

Access to the internet is heavily influenced by policies enacted by various governments. According to Adadevoh [68], the willingness of the government and their emphasis on closing the digital gap may be credited with the spread of information and communication technologies in Ghana. As a result, the government of Ghana has expended a significant amount of effort toward the establishment of e-commerce-oriented and enabling regulations in order to foster an information and communications technology (ICT) environment that is advantageous for enterprises [71]. Between the years 2006 and 2014, the E-Transform Ghana Project provided help to the government of Ghana in the implementation of its agenda for ICT-led development. This assistance was awarded as a result of the government of Ghana's request. As a direct consequence of the completion of this project, the International Development Association was able to fulfil its obligation to give funds in the amount of US $80.25 million [35]. The ICT for Accelerated Growth policy was put into effect by the government to accelerate the country's socio-economic development. This was the first step in the government's plan [68]. The use of e-commerce as a method of product marketing is being encouraged by governments worldwide *via* the implementation of laws that foster the expansion of information and communications technologies (ICT). The growth of the nation's information and communications technology (ICT) sector is being aided by the international community. The efforts of the Ghanaian government regarding ICT projects have been successful so far, which may be attributed to the assistance that has been provided by several UN agencies and foreign donors, who continue to provide that support [71]. Existing information and communication technology (ICT) projects in Ghana include ICT training centres, an e-government portal that facilitates interactions between the government and its constituents, and the general public, and support for ICT initiatives from the International Institute for Communication and Development.

SMEs and E-commerce

People who live and work in other countries have a significant role in the dissemination of innovative technology, particularly small to medium-sized firms. According to Choshin and Ghaffari , the most significant issues facing the sector of e-commerce are maintaining satisfied clients, putting in place the appropriate infrastructure at the most cost-effective price, and ensuring that people are aware of and comprehending e-commerce. There are a variety of causes that might lead to an increase in the usage of e-commerce. Some of these factors include: technological prowess; management strategies; business strategies; the needs for both customers and suppliers; and other aspects. When Ghanaian expats return to their home country, they are able to effectively integrate e-commerce into the manner that they conduct their enterprises because of the education and business skills that they gained while living in industrialized nations. They do this by using educational experiences garnered from developed countries. When using e-commerce as a method of product promotion, owners of SME businesses need to have a working understanding of IT abilities.

According to research by Boateng *et al.*, many Ghanaian SME owners possess the technical expertise to develop original ICT-based strategies for the expansion and sustainability of their businesses. Amourest Consult, I-Net Ghana, and Broadband Home are just a few of the Ghanaian consultancies that cater to SMEs with information and communications technology (ICT) services. Businesses in some sectors can improve their capacity for innovation and promote e-commerce by either contracting out their information technology operations or hiring trained employees.

The tactic of making use of the expertise of experts can prove to be beneficial, especially with regard to the situation in Ghana. Despite the sluggish adoption of online commerce among SMEs, the number of internet users in Ghana has expanded. The consequence is that Ghana has undergone extraordinary development in the penetration of information and communication technologies in every sector of the economy, and the blossoming influence that this expansion has had on the importance of societal and economic pursuits cannot be overstated [71]. SME owners in Ghana, according to Addo, are still unwilling to fully incorporate e-commerce into their company operations, despite the many advantages it may provide. The absence of the owner's knowledge and competence in information technology might give rise to concerns over the potential of e-commerce technology to disrupt the operations of the firm [72].

Theory

TAM Model

Davis initially proposed the TAM in 1989 as a rationale for embracing new technologies. Davis created the model by combining the theories of rational action and planned conduct with the new notions of PEOU and PU [73]. The TAM is the most reliable hypothesis for predicting how people will respond to a new IT system. People's attitudes toward technology may influence whether or not they intend to utilize new technology, according to research using the TAM. Perceived ease of use and perceived utility, which Davis [37] predicted by utilizing earlier data from multiple disciplines, demonstrate people's intention of adopting new technology. Using 40 participants, Davis [37] found that PEOU and PU impact computer users' intentions to employ new technology.

TAM focuses on whether or not a certain technology is accepted or rejected by users [73]. As a result of two major constructs: (a) whether users believe the system will help them improve their performance; and (b) whether they believe the system is simple to use [37]. Adoption choices may be tested by observing users' behavior and attitudes toward. The more a user views the technology's utility and simplicity of use, the more likely the user is to adopt the technology. Results demonstrated that the new IT's usefulness outweighed its ease of use [37].

New technology adoption may be examined by focusing on PU and PEOU. Several plausible ideas may be used to estimate the degree to which consumers' habits are adjusting to accommodate internet shopping. When it comes to how many different sectors may benefit from using IT solutions, TAM is the best concept (Dong *et al.*, 2017). Therefore, the TAM offers a solid theoretical grounding for anticipating the actions of online shoppers. These two concepts were the foundation of the study analysis conducted by Hidayat-ur- Rehman *et al.* [106], Wang, Wang, and Liu to predict how often a user would make purchases using an e-commerce platform.

Conceptual Framework

Ease of use and OSI

The amount of effort that a user of a piece of technology has to put out in order to utilize it effectively is known as the "perceived ease of use," or simply "ease of use" [37]. In this particular research, PEOU was shown to be connected with the amount of ease that one feels while making purchases *via* the use of EC platforms. Consumers regularly express their dissatisfaction with the amount of time and effort required to do activities such as looking for products, viewing available options, and making a purchase on an e-commerce website. It is a common issue among customers who have walked away from their purchases on EC websites because they were unable to find the product they wanted [74]. It is necessary for the platform to possess specific traits in order for the shopper's process of making decisions to be simplified. When a user searches on the platform, it should provide appropriate search assistance (such as *via* a search engine), make suggestions that are pertinent in response to that search, and arrange the contents (including goods) efficiently. When these efforts are done, it will be possible to enhance the function and design of the EC platform, which will ultimately lead to an increased sense of ease of use on the part of online consumers. Based on the above assertion, we hypothesize that:

H1: There is a significant positive relationship between the perceived ease of use and consumer online shopping behavior (Fig. **1**).

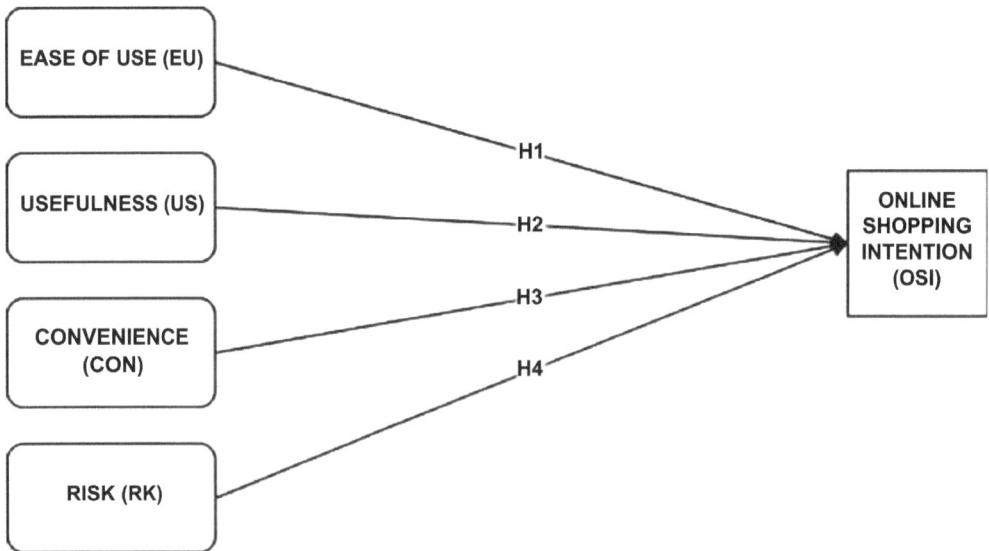

Fig. (1). Path analysis.

Usefulness and OSI

Davis [37] argues that shoppers' impressions of value have a role in whether or not they make a purchase. The perceived utility of a system is defined as the confidence with which a potential user feels that using that system would improve his or her performance [75]. Perceived usefulness in the context of online purchasing is the extent to which an individual shopper feels that doing so would increase their shopping efficiency [52]. There is data suggesting that a consumer's perception of value plays a key role in determining whether or not they would make a purchase online [52, 75, 76]. Therefore, the second proposed hypothesis is:

H2: There is a significant positive relationship between perceived usefulness and consumer online shopping behaviour.

Convenience and OSI

Consumers in the online buying environment are motivated by the utilitarian benefits of online purchases [77]. The ease of online shopping is an excellent illustration of a utilitarian advantage [78]. It is easy to compare prices and save time while buying online since it's possible to purchase from any place and save time [79, 80]. A large percentage of the population is busy with their daily routines and is severely limited in their ability to go shopping in person [78]. Because of this, many see internet shopping as a way to save time [79]. As previously stated, the elimination of travel time and long lines is a major convenience factor that encourages individuals to purchase online in large numbers, as previously stated [81]. Convenience is an important consideration in this study for two reasons. The first reason is that many individuals value convenience. The growth of e-commerce has been heavily influenced by the importance of convenience in the past, and this is still the case now [82]. First and foremost, ease is often recognized as a major benefit of buying products online [83]. Convenience is more important to online customers than to conventional purchasers, according to research by Korgaonkar *et al*. [84].

Convenience is the driving force for internet shopping, according to an extensive study [81]. In their research, Cho and Sagynov (2015) found that consumers' willingness to make an online purchase improves as their opinion of the convenience of doing so grows. It is possible to compare several items at any time and from any location, which contributes to convenience [85, 80]. Anesbury *et al*. [81] also examined the favorable influence of convenience on online shopping as opposed to the difficulties of going to brick-and-mortar shops in pursuit of the desired item. According to Tandon *et al*. [86], customers' willingness to purchase online is influenced by the ease with which they may order products online. According to Korgaonkar *et al*. [84], buyers that prioritize convenience are more likely to make an online purchase. The following hypothesis is proposed as a result:

H3: There is a significant positive relationship between perceived convenience and consumer online shopping behavior.

Risk and OSI

The term "perceived risk" refers to the customers' impressions of both the unpredictability and the potentially bad outcomes of their participation in particular activities [52]. Mayer *et al.* [87] suggest that risk perception is the consumers' impression of the likelihood of gaining or losing money in transactions with retailers or distributors. This is a more precise definition of risk perception. When consumers purchase online, rather than making direct contact with vendors, they utilize the internet to contact them. This presents several potential dangers. When compared to purchases made in physical stores, making purchases online is connected with an increased likelihood of exposing one's finances to danger due to rising customer worries about the security of their credit cards and identities being stolen [88]. However, Bezes *et al.* [89] performed research in which they compared shoppers' views of the dangers of brick-and-mortar stores to those of online retailers. The overall, logistical, psychological, and performance risks were shown to be more prevalent for online purchasing, whereas the financial and time risks were found to be marginally greater for in-store purchases. It is not surprising that the number of individuals who shop online would decrease if both the payment risk and the product risk coefficient had negative signals, as reported by Alnsour *et al.* [90]. For products where tactile experience is paramount, perceived product risk is more influential than any other factor in determining whether or not consumers would make purchases online. It was shown that consumers were most influenced by their perception of the product's inherent risk, such as the difficulty in judging the quality of an item purchased online. The following is the hypothesis that is being put forward:

H4: Perceived risk has a negative relationship with customers' online shopping intention.

METHODOLOGY

Research Design

The study employed a quantitative method. All three types of experiments, as well as the quasi-experimental and non-experimental correlational, descriptive, and evaluative methodologies, make up the spectrum of quantitative designs [91]. The most suitable quantitative strategy for this investigation was a survey. When assessing two or more quantitative variables from the same set of participants to establish a link between those variables, researchers should employ a survey design, as suggested by Bettany-Saltikov and Whittaker (2014) [92]. As a result, we used this approach to investigate the correlation between various online elements (the independent variables) and the outcome of interest (the dependent variable, online buying intentions).

Population and Sample Size

Study participants were at least 18 years old online shoppers in Tamale, Ghana, who have engaged in online shopping for at least 2 years. A convenient sampling technique was used to select a sample of three hundred (300) respondents from the population in order to obtain the information needed to help the study accomplish its objectives. It means data was taken from shoppers available. Convenience sampling is cheaper and faster [91]. Due to the nature of the Tamale online shoppers and the fact that the population was difficult to define and is spread all over the municipality, a convenient sampling technique was more appropriate. The years of online shopping experience were used as a selection criterion to help the appreciation of the subject under consideration by the participants.

Data Collection Technique

To acquire quantitative data, online surveys are a quick and dependable option [93]. In order to avoid the poor response and completion rates and high costs associated with traditional survey methods like paper, email, and social media, we used the Qualtrics website to collect our data. Online surveys are a popular method of collecting data because of its accessibility, speed, cheap cost, convenience, and quick turnaround time [94, 95]. Low response rates, sample bias, difficulty to reach those with restricted Internet access, and the likelihood of survey fraud are all possible issues with online surveys [96]. The fact that respondents may stop answering questions at any moment is another drawback of online surveys [96]. After weighing the benefits and downsides of various data gathering techniques, management researchers often use online questionnaires [94]. When doing quantitative research, online surveys are the most efficient and reliable option, as stated by Bryman and Bell [97]. The reliability and validity of a research are bolstered when a previously developed instrument is used [98 - 100]. A pilot study is a smaller-scale research project used to test the feasibility of a larger study in terms of resources (such as time and money), statistical variance, and accuracy of predictions [101].

Instrument of Data Collection

Questionnaires, interviews, focus groups, surveys, and observations are data collection instruments. Even though data collection can be done with a variety of tools, the nature, and type of research determine which instrument should be used. The basic device for obtaining data from online shoppers was a questionnaire. A five-point Likert scale was employed in the study. The following scales were used by participants to indicate their level of agreement or disagreement with each of the statements: 1 = strong disagreement, 2 = disagreement, 3 = neutrality, 4 = agreement, and 5 = strong agreement [102].

Data Analysis

For Windows, IBM SPSS 25.0 and Amos 24.0 are statistical and graphical data analysis packages [103]. Using a combination of descriptive statistics, Pearson's correlation analysis, and structural equation modelling, this programme can provide a comprehensive overview of data distributions in terms of both frequency and percentage [103]. Direct and indirect correlations between various independent and dependent variables in big datasets may be evaluated and predicted with the help of AMOS. SPSS-Amos was used to investigate the links between the extrinsic and dependent elements of consumers' intentions to shop online and the independent factors of the online adoption factors components. Participant answers were used to support or disprove four different theories. Independent and dependent variables are distinguished, as well as their interrelationships, in a discussion presented by Li, Chen, and Zhang (2020). They also check the level of predictability between the outcome and the explanatory factors.

Measures of central trends, such as minimums, means, maximums, and standard deviations, may be found using descriptive statistics [103]. In order to construct the general distribution of a variable, knowing its frequency and percentage level is helpful [103]. Examination of the survey's demographics and the development of a graphical depiction of the correlation between survey answers and study parameters were both accomplished by use of descriptive statistics. Bryman and Bell [97], claims that blanks are inevitable in computer-assisted polls. All unfinished surveys were discarded from the analysis to make room for data gaps.

MEASURES

Demographic Data

The first part of the questionnaire is made of demographic factors such as age, gender, occupation *etc.*

Independent Variable

The independent variables are the factors predicting online shopping behavior. These factors comprised 14 items derived from the constructs (convenience, utility, ease of utilization, and perceived risk) as outlined by Jiang *et al.* [104]. The least Cronbach's alpha value for these scales was 0.79 for this study. All items were measured using a 5-point Likert-type scale (1 = strongly disagree and 5 = strongly agree).

Dependent Variable

This study looked at how likely people were to online shopping intention (OSI). Shephard *et al.* [105] made a scale with three statements that was used to measure how likely people were to shop online (*e.g.*, If I were going shopping, I would likely shop online). In this study, the alpha for this scale was 0.83. All of the questions were answered on a 5-point Likert scale, where 1 means strongly disagree and 5 means strongly agree.

DATA ANALYSIS AND RESULTS

Demographic Data

Data was collected from 300 respondents, but after data cleaning 240 responses were used to run the analysis. In Table **1** below, we assessed the demographics based on gender, age, occupation and monthly overall income of the respondents. It was found that many female shop online than male in Ghana since 62.5% of the respondents were female and only 37.5% were male. When it comes to age of the respondents, Ghanaians whose ages ranged from 31 to 50 were involve in online shopping than other ages, after all, 100(41.7%) were scored respectively for age 31-40 and from 41-50 years. Only 30(12.5%) were between the ages of 20-30 years, whilst 10(4.1%) were between the ages of 51-60. The respondents' income were also assessed. 103(42.9%) and 102(42.5%) of the respondents earn between 500-2000 and 1100-4000 Ghana Cedis a month. However, those who earn more are small in Ghana. For instance, 20(8.3%) of the respondents earn between GH₵5100-7000, whilst those who earn between 7100-10,000 were just 15(6.25%). Hence, the purchasing power of Ghanaians are relatively small.

Table 1. Loadings, Average Variance Extracted (AVE), and Composite Reliability (CR).

Variables	Items	Loadings	A	CR	AVE
Ease of use	EU1	0.77	0.88	0.78	0.68
-	EU2	0.71	-	-	-
-	EU3	0.77	-	-	-
-	EU4	0.76	-	-	-
-	EU5	0.82	-	-	-
Usefulness	-	-	0.89	0.82	0.63
-	US1	0.81	-	-	-

Variables	Items	Loadings	A	CR	AVE
-	US2	0.75	-	-	-
-	US3	0.70	-	-	-
-	US4	0.72	-	-	-
Convenience	-	-	0.92	0.85	0.59
-	CON1	0.78	-	-	-
-	CON2	0.85	-	-	-
-	CON3	0.74	-	-	-
-	CON4	0.83	-	-	-
-	CON5	0.77	-	-	-
Risk	-	-	0.93	0.88	0.56
-	RK1	0.72	-	-	-
-	RK2	0.74	0.86	0.92	0.65
-	RK3	0.81	-	-	-
-	RK4	0.77	-	-	-

RELIABILITY AND VALIDITY

Convergent Validity

The degree to which all items of a construct measure the specific construct(s) is referred to as convergent validity [106]. According to Hair Jr, Hult, Ringle, and Sarstedt [107], convergent validity examines three things: average variance-extracted (AVE), factor loadings, and composite reliability (CR). To acquire the greatest CR and AVE results, we excluded all elements with a factor loading of less than 0.50%. This study met the AVE and factor loading criteria, as shown in Table **2**.

Table 2. Discriminant validity.

Variables	AVE	EU	US	CON	RK	OSI
EU	0.68	**0.82**	-	-	-	-
US	0.63	0.67	**0.79**	-	-	-
CON	0.59	0.58	0.64	**0.77**	-	-
RK	0.56	0.69	0.66	0.70	**0.75**	-
OSI	0.65	0.55	0.54	0.65	0.72	**0.81**

Two of the testing criteria that are considered to be essential in order to establish the reliability of a measuring scale are the items-to-total correlations [108] and Cronbach's Alpha [109]. Both of these citations were written by Cronbach. If the item-to-total correlation is at least 0.7 and the Cronbach's Alpha value is more than 0.7, the scale can be used in research. Crosbach's Alpha value [107]. Every one of the variables has alpha values that are superior to the minimum required standard. The fit indices of Cronbach's Alpha are excellent when measured against the threshold level. This is because Cronbach's Alpha produces exceptionally accurate results. The essential criteria for CR (more than 0.70) and AVE (0.50) are shown in Table **2** [107]. This research satisfied the requirements set out by Nunnally (1978), which stated that the value of Cronbach's alpha needed to be 0.70 or greater than 0.70.

Discriminant Validity

Discriminant validity is a circumstance in which researchers see that every indication of a theoretical model differs from one another in terms of statistical significance [106]. The discriminant validity of this study was evaluated in accordance with the recommendations of Fornell and Larcker [110]. It is possible to compute discriminant validity by employing one of the methods. First, the values of the AVE square root were compared to the values of the correlation coefficient. Second, the AVE was compared to correlations that were squared. For the purposes of this investigation, the first approach was utilized to compute discriminant validity. The value of the AVE square root in the upper diagonals must be greater than the value of the AVE square root in corresponding rows and columns in Table **3** below.

Table 3. Hypothesis testing.

Paths	Hypothesis	t-values	β	p-values	Decision
EU → OSI	H1	12.85	0.562	0.000	Supported
US → OSI	H2	11.02	0.541	0.001	Supported
CON → OSI	H3	9.83	0.352	0.005	Supported
RK → OSI	H4	12.09	0.552	0.000	Supported
Sig	*0.000*	-	-	-	-
R^2	*0.577*	-	-	-	-

In this study, criterion-related validity was established by correlating the four independent variables with the dependent variable, which was the intention to shop online. All four characteristics, namely convenience (0.65), ease of use (0.55), usefulness (0.54), and risk (0.72), exhibit statistically significant positive relationships with online shopping intention, as illustrated in Table **4** and Fig. (**2**) below.

Table 4. Variables, Items, and Source.

Perceived Ease of Use [104]
PEOU1 Using social media is intuitive for me.
PEOU2 I can easily see and understand how to use social media.
PEOU3 I find it easy to use social media.
PEOU4 It does not take much work to use social media.
Usefulness [104].
US1. My favourite online stores make it easy for me to buy things quickly.
US2. My favourite online stores make it easier to find information.
US3. It helps me to shop at my favourite online stores.
US4. My favourite online stores have transactions that are good for me.
Perceived Risk [104]
RK1. Before making purchases online, it is important to look at other options.
RK2. Buying things on the internet with a credit card is safe.
RK3. If the products are good, it would not matter if you gave your credit card information over the web.
Convenience [104]
CON1. I felt secure to submit my personal and confidential details.
CON2. I had no trouble getting the information I needed to decide what to buy.
CON3. Could buy things whenever I wanted.
CON4. The online store cared about me as an individual.
Online Shopping Intention [104].
OSI1. If I were to make a purchase, I may consider purchasing the item online.
OSI2. If I were to shop, I would most likely do it online.
OSI3. Most likely, I will shop online.

source: Field data (2023).

Among all the independent variables, ease of use (EU) is revealed to be the most dominant factor impacting online shopping intention, with the highest Beta value and p-value (= 0.562, p=0.000), followed by convenience (0.176), time saving (0.163), and web design/features (0.132). As a result, in this study, ease of use is the most important predictor. In other words, when the p-value is less than 0.01 independent factors are strongly associated with the dependent variable.

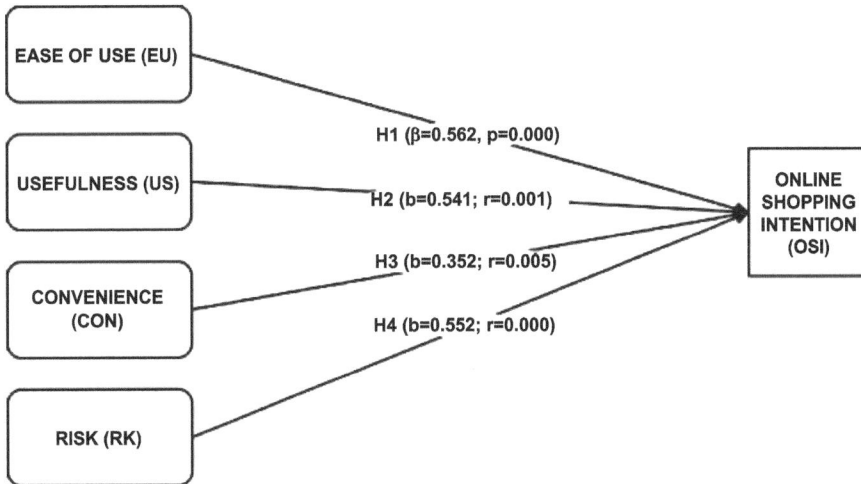

Fig. (2). Hypothesis testing.

Every factor of online motives was treated as an independent variable in Table **4**. These dimensions account for 57.7% of online purchase intent, according to the R 2 value. Convenience (= 0.352; = 0.005), usefulness (= 0. 541; = 0.001), and perceived risk (= 0.552; = 0.000) are the variables that have the greatest impact on online purchase intention. These findings, which are all statistically significant (0.05), provide answers to research issues.

SUMMARY OF FINDINGS

Every aspect of online motivations was considered in the independent variables. These dimensions account for 57.7% of online purchase intent, according to the R2 value. Convenience (= 0.352; = 0.005), usefulness (= 0. 541; = 0.001), and perceived risk (= 0.552; = 0.000) are the variables that have the greatest impact on online purchase intention. These findings, which are all statistically significant (0.05), provide answers to research issues.

CONCLUSION

Based on an examination of relevant past research conducted as part of this inquiry, the results of this study revealed the most essential characteristics of consumers' behaviour that should be considered when generating predictions about their intentions to make online purchases of products and services. This research not only sheds insight into the potential and function of these factors in the explosion and growth of online shopping, notably in Ghana, but it also sheds light on the critical repercussions from the findings. Furthermore, the study resulted in the creation of a framework that would aid online merchants in better understanding the desires that online consumers will have in the future. Given the prevalence of online shopping in Ghana, it is critical to understand the factors that influence client intents and the degree to which the activity is permitted. As a result, the findings will be useful to online merchants in developing methods that will keep consumers interested in continuing to recognize internet buying as a viable choice. It is critical for all parties engaged in this expanding industry to perform market research, especially at this time when internet retail is still in its early phases of growth. This is important in order to assure the growing company's long-term prosperity. As a result, the growth and usage of online shopping will result in the availability of a broad range of items among consumers, ultimately leading to an improvement in the customers' standard of living while also increasing GDP. Nonetheless, the construction of a conceptual framework has resulted in a significant contribution to theory as a consequence of this study. As a result, a request has been made for more research to be conducted in order to empirically analyze the model in order to determine whether or not it is accurate and valid.

IMPLICATION OF THE STUDY

This research identifies many growing themes that, if adopted by SMEs and their management, might increase retail e-commerce sales. Three main ideas have emerged from this study: (a) using social media for marketing; (b) utilising government SME online business certification systems; and (c) selling through third-party online retailers. As a result of our review into the relevant literature and examination of the available data, we have developed three suggestions that small and medium-sized enterprises (SMEs) may use in order to increase the amount of money they make *via* retail internet commerce. The first piece of advice that I would provide is to encourage them to make use of social media in order to attract clients to their firm. To successfully market their goods and services, small and medium-sized enterprises (SMEs) need to ascertain which social media channels are the most well-liked by the demographic of users they are trying to reach and then use those channels. The government of Ghana cites Instagram, WhatsApp, and Snapchat as some of the most widely used social media sites in the country. However, a social networking site that is popular in one nation could not be popular in another one, and vice versa. When utilising social media platforms as a promotional tool, small and medium-sized enterprises (SMEs) have the opportunity to try to improve consumer loyalty among their target market. As a direct consequence of this, small and medium-sized businesses (SMEs) in Ghana have the opportunity to boost the level of confidence and confidentiality enjoyed by their clientele by registering on official government websites. Platforms for social media on the internet can also be beneficial to small and medium-sized businesses (SMEs) because they allow for two-way communication with customers, which allows for the evaluation of customer feedback regarding the company's various products, offers, and services, amongst other things. Abed [111], investigated what variables affect consumers' propensity to make a purchase in Ghana. Abed found that the two most significant elements impacting the purchase decisions of Ghanaian consumers were social influence, especially on Instagram, and trust. Based on what was uncovered, small and medium-sized enterprises (SMEs) in Ghana could use a combination of this study's and Abed's findings to develop a strategy that involves (a) registering on Maroof websites to gain customers' trust and (b) using the Instagram platform to influence consumers' purchasing inclinations. The second piece of advice is for SMEs to think about promoting their goods and services *via* third-party online shops.

Third-party online retailers have become more popular, which might be good news for SMEs looking to broaden their customer base. Managers of small and medium sized enterprises (SMEs) might potentially benefit from the expertise of a third-party online shop. Small and medium-sized enterprises (SMEs) may enter the e-commerce market by forming strategic alliances with established players like Amazon and Noon. Small and medium-sized enterprises (SMEs) might benefit from opening their own online shops if they have gained expertise in electronic commerce. In the future, however, we advise that they make use of external web-based firms as a new channel for sales. If a small or medium-sized firm (SME) is still in its formative stages and lacks the personnel with expertise in internet marketing and advertising, it may seek the guidance of a third-party online retailer. Our third piece of advice for SMEs is to think about the three themes that came out of this research and figure out the best way to combine them based on their strengths and the markets they want to reach. SME owners and managers can also market their businesses by using social media sites like Instagram and Snapchat, as well as a mix of online shops like Amazon and Noon. Small and medium-sized businesses (SMEs) should join a group of social media platforms and third-party online storefronts to boost their retail e-commerce sales. Researchers share their findings in reputable academic journals so that they can add to what is already known [112].

FUTURE RESEARCH

Future research should expand its scope to include other parts, especially in rural areas of Ghana, as the current study focused mostly on Tamale in the country's northern region. The Ghanaian government will be better able to understand the challenges they face in terms of knowledge about online shopping, internet line connection, and development, as well as how to improve their information technology (IT) so that they do not become obsolete, by expanding the scope of the research to include rural areas.

Future researchers could add another variable, such as price, so that the data can be used by online marketers to better understand how cost affects customer perceptions while shopping online, among other things. Future research could look into what other issues buyers may have, such as undelivered goods or services, obtaining the wrong product, and currency exchange while buying from foreign countries. We discovered in this study that online marketers, particularly new marketers and sellers, can utilize this study as knowledge and a guide to assist them to open up their enterprises and build their market in order to compete with others in the future. Aside from that, internet vendors and marketers must understand the attributes that clients seek. Online vendors must also be abreast of current events in the world, especially in terms of security. They must address the issue as quickly as possible by deploying a good antivirus product and establishing a security homepage to make it more difficult for hackers to steal user information and identities. It would be interesting to do qualitative research in the future utilising interviews and focus groups to better understand additional factors and to expand the complexity and depth of the analysis, given that this study is strictly quantitative.

REFERENCES

[1]   Sabou S, Avram-Pop B, Zima LA. The impact of the problems faced by online customers on ecommerce. Studia Universitatis Babes-Bolyai Oeconomica 2017; 62(2): 77-88.
        [http://dx.doi.org/10.1515/subboec-2017-0010]

[2]   Awiagah R, Kang J, Lim JI. Factors affecting e-commerce adoption among SMEs in Ghana. Inf Dev 2016; 32(4): 815-36.
        [http://dx.doi.org/10.1177/0266666915571427]

[3]   Isohella L, Oikarinen EL, Saarela M, Muhos M, Nikunen T. Perceptions of digital marketing tools in new microenterprises. Proceedings of the MakeLearn and TIIM International Conference. Vol. 85: 95.

[4]   Kim K, Kim S, Park CY. Food Security in Asia and the Pacific amid the COVID-19 Pandemic 2020.
        [http://dx.doi.org/10.22617/BRF200176-2]

[5]   Kumar D, Dange U. A study of factors affecting online buying behavior: A conceptual model. Ujwala, A Study of Factors Affecting Online Buying Behavior: A Conceptual Model 2012.

[6]   Gabriel J, Ogbuigwe T, Ahiauzu L. Online shopping systems in Nigeria: Evolution, trend and prospects. Asian Research Journal of Arts & Social Sciences 2016; 1(4): 1-7.
        [http://dx.doi.org/10.9734/ARJASS/2016/29170]

[7]   Omotayo FO, Omotope AR. Determinants of continuance intention to use online shops in Nigeria. J Internet Bank Commerce 2018; 23(2): 1-48.

[8]   Fayad R, Paper D. The technology acceptance model e-commerce extension: A conceptual framework. Procedia Econ Finance 2015; 26: 1000-6.
        [http://dx.doi.org/10.1016/S2212-5671(15)00922-3]

[9]   Singh P, Keswani S, Singh S, Sharma S. A study of adoption behavior for online shopping: an

extension of TAM model. IJASSH 2018.

[10]   Venkatesh V, Thong JY, Xu X. Consumer acceptance and use of information technology: Extending the unified theory of acceptance and use of technology. Manage Inf Syst Q 2012; 36(1): 157-78.
[http://dx.doi.org/10.2307/41410412]

[11]   Ayodele AA, Ifeanyichukwu C. Factors influencing smartphone purchase behavior among young adults in Nigeria. Int J Recent Sci Res 2016; 7: 13248-54.

[12]   Rahman MS, Mannan M. Consumer online purchase behavior of local fashion clothing brands. J Fash Mark Manag 2018; 22(3): 404-19.
[http://dx.doi.org/10.1108/JFMM-11-2017-0118]

[13]   Butt A, Ahmad H, Muzaffar A, Ali F, Shafique N. WOW, the make-up AR app is impressive: A comparative study between China and South Korea. J Serv Mark 2022; 36(1): 73-88.
[http://dx.doi.org/10.1108/JSM-12-2020-0508]

[14]   Leonardi PM, Bailey DE, Diniz EH, Sholler D, Nardi B. Multiplex appropriation in complex systems implementation: The case of brazil's correspondent banking system. Manage Inf Syst Q 2016; 40(2): 461-73.
[http://dx.doi.org/10.25300/MISQ/2016/40.2.10]

[15]   Agwu EM, Murray PJ. Empirical study of barriers to electronic commerce adoption by small and medium scale businesses in Nigeria. Int J Innov Digit Econ 2015; 6(2): 1-19.
[http://dx.doi.org/10.4018/ijide.2015040101]

[16]   Nwankwo CA, Kanyangale M, Abugu JO. Online shopping industry and its consumers in Nigeria. *Journal of Economics*. Management and Trade 2019; 24(3): 1-12.

[17]   Yang Q, Pang C, Liu L, Yen DC, Michael Tarn J. Exploring consumer perceived risk and trust for online payments: An empirical study in China's younger generation. Comput Human Behav 2015; 50: 9-24.
[http://dx.doi.org/10.1016/j.chb.2015.03.058]

[18]   Pei Y, Wang S, Fan J, Zhang M. An empirical study on the impact of perceived benefit, risk and trust on e-payment adoption: Comparing quick pay and union pay in China. In 2015 7th international conference on intelligent human-machine systems and cybernetics 2015; 2: 198-202.

[19]   Khan SA, Liang Y, Shahzad S. An empirical study of perceived factors affecting customer satisfaction to re-purchase intention in online stores in China. J Serv Sci Manag 2015; 8(3): 291-305.
[http://dx.doi.org/10.4236/jssm.2015.83032]

[20]   Nguyen DH, de Leeuw S, Dullaert WEH. Consumer behaviour and order fulfilment in online retailing: A systematic review. Int J Manag Rev 2018; 20(2): 255-76.
[http://dx.doi.org/10.1111/ijmr.12129]

[21]   Rao S, Rabinovich E, Raju D. The role of physical distribution services as determinants of product returns in Internet retailing. J Oper Manage 2014; 32(6): 295-312.
[http://dx.doi.org/10.1016/j.jom.2014.06.005]

[22]   Kabir AA, Musibau AA. Adoption of electronic commerce technology in emerging nations: A conceptual review of the literature. *International Journal of Economics*. Commerce and Management 2018; 2(1): 455-72.

[23]   Alatawy K. From offline to online: Do saudis change their information search behaviour? Economic and Social Development: Book of Proceedings, 2018; 15-27.

[24]   Ezzi SW. Exploring the characteristics of the e-commerce marketplace in Saudi Arabia. International Journal of Economic Perspectives 2016; 10(4): 5-20.

[25]   Zafar A, Mustafa S. SMEs and its role in economic and socio-economic development of Pakistan. International Journal of Academic Research in Accounting, Finance and Management Sciences, 2017; 6(4).

[26]   Bouazza AB. Small and medium enterprises as an effective sector for economic development and employment creation in Algeria. International Journal of Economics, commerce and management, 2015; 3(2): 1-16.

[27]   Fiseha GG, Oyelana AA. An assessment of the roles of small and medium enterprises (SMEs) in the local economic development (LED). S Afr J Econ 2015; 6(3): 280-90.

[28]   Muriithi Samuel Muiruri. African small and medium enterprises (SMEs) contributions, challenges and solutions 2017; 5(1).

[29]   Aga G, Francis DC, Meza JR. SMEs, age, and jobs: A review of the literature, metrics, and evidence. World Bank Policy Res Work Pap 2015; 7493.
[http://dx.doi.org/10.1596/1813-9450-7493]

[30]   Katua NT. The role of SMEs in employment creation and economic growth in selected countries. Int J Educ Res (Dhaka) 2014; 2(12): 461-72.

[31]   Ayyagari M, Demirguc-Kunt A, Maksimovic V. Who creates jobs in developing countries? Small Bus Econ 2014; 43(1): 75-99.
[http://dx.doi.org/10.1007/s11187-014-9549-5]

[32]   Ndiaye N, Abdul Razak L, Nagayev R, Ng A. Demystifying small and medium enterprises' (SMEs) performance in emerging and developing economies. Borsa Istanbul Review 2018; 18(4): 269-81.
[http://dx.doi.org/10.1016/j.bir.2018.04.003]

[33]   Prempeh KB. Problems of financing SMEs in Ghana: A case study of the Sunyani municipality. Journal of Advance Research in Business Management and Accounting 2015; 1(1): 28-47.

[34]   Quartey P, Turkson E, Abor JY, Iddrisu AM. Financing the growth of SMEs in Africa: What are the contraints to SME financing within ECOWAS? Review of development finance 2017; 7(1): 18-28.

[35]   World Bank Group. World development report 2016: Digital dividends. World Bank Publications 2016.

[36]   Pierre A, Fernandez AS. Going deeper into SMEs' innovation capacity: An empirical exploration of innovation capacity factors. Journal of Innovation Economics 2018; 25(1): 139-81.
[http://dx.doi.org/10.3917/jie.pr1.0019]

[37]   Davis FD. Perceived usefulness, perceived ease of use, and user acceptance of information technology. Manage Inf Syst Q 1989; 13(3): 319.
[http://dx.doi.org/10.2307/249008]

[38]   Osama S, Naderpour M. Decision making on adoption of cloud computing in e-commerce using fuzzy TOPSIS. 2017 IEEE International Conference on Fuzzy Systems (FUZZ-IEEE) 2017; 1-6.

[39]   Venkatesh V, Morris MG, Davis GB, Davis FD. User acceptance of information technology: Toward a unified view. Manage Inf Syst Q 2003; 27(3): 425-78.
[http://dx.doi.org/10.2307/30036540]

[40]   Park CH, Kim YG. Identifying key factors affecting consumer purchase behavior in an online shopping context. Int J Retail Distrib Manag 2003; 31(1): 16-29.
[http://dx.doi.org/10.1108/09590550310457818]

[41]   Alalwan AA, Dwivedi YK, Rana NP, Algharabat R. Examining factors influencing Jordanian customers' intentions and adoption of internet banking: Extending UTAUT2 with risk. J Retailing Consum Serv 2018; 40: 125-38.
[http://dx.doi.org/10.1016/j.jretconser.2017.08.026]

[42]   Gong W, Stump RL, Maddox LM. Factors influencing consumers' online shopping in China. J Asia Bus Stud 2013; 7(3): 214-30.
[http://dx.doi.org/10.1108/JABS-02-2013-0006]

[43]   Lian JW, Yen DC. Online shopping drivers and barriers for older adults: Age and gender differences.

Comput Human Behav 2014; 37: 133-43.
[http://dx.doi.org/10.1016/j.chb.2014.04.028]

[44]   Weerasinghe CAK, Kumar S. Intention to pursue overseas jobs among university students and graduates: a case study from University of Peradeniya, Sri Lanka. Tropical Agricultural Research 2014; 26(1): 94-108.
[http://dx.doi.org/10.4038/tar.v26i1.8075]

[45]   Chen G, Mei F. Research on the willingness to accept mobile internet advertising based on customer perception---a case of college students. 2017.

[46]   Elkhani N, Soltani S, Jamshidi MHM. Examining a hybrid model for e-satisfaction and e-loyalty to e-ticketing on airline websites. J Air Transp Manage 2014; 37: 36-44.
[http://dx.doi.org/10.1016/j.jairtraman.2014.01.006]

[47]   Bhatiasevi V, Yoopetch C. The determinants of intention to use electronic booking among young users in Thailand. J Hosp Tour Manag 2015; 23: 1-11.
[http://dx.doi.org/10.1016/j.jhtm.2014.12.004]

[48]   Kim J, Park J. A consumer shopping channel extension model: Attitude shift toward the online store. J Fash Mark Manag 2005; 9(1): 106-21.
[http://dx.doi.org/10.1108/13612020510586433]

[49]   Lee YH, Hsieh YC, Hsu CN. Adding innovation diffusion theory to the technology acceptance model: supporting employees' intentions to use E-learning systems. J Educ Technol Soc 2011; 14(4): 124-37.

[50]   Hsieh LY, Lu YJ, Lee YH. Using the technology acceptance model to explore the behavioral intentions toward blended learning. International Workshop on Learning Technology for Education in Cloud 2014; 195-203.
[http://dx.doi.org/10.1007/978-3-319-10671-7_20]

[51]   Lee YK, Park JH, Chung N, Blakeney A. A unified perspective on the factors influencing usage intention toward mobile financial services. J Bus Res 2012; 65(11): 1590-9.
[http://dx.doi.org/10.1016/j.jbusres.2011.02.044]

[52]   Ha NT. The impact of perceived risk on consumers' online shopping intention: An integration of TAM and TPB. Management Science Letters 2020; 10(9): 2029-36.
[http://dx.doi.org/10.5267/j.msl.2020.2.009]

[53]   Ramayah T, Lo MC. Impact of shared beliefs on "perceived usefulness" and "ease of use" in the implementation of an enterprise resource planning system. Manage Res News 2007; 30(6): 420-31.
[http://dx.doi.org/10.1108/01409170710751917]

[54]   Luarn P, Lin HH. Toward an understanding of the behavioral intention to use mobile banking. Comput Human Behav 2005; 21(6): 873-91.
[http://dx.doi.org/10.1016/j.chb.2004.03.003]

[55]   Verhoef PC, Neslin SA, Vroomen B. Multichannel customer management: Understanding the research-shopper phenomenon. Int J Res Mark 2007; 24(2): 129-48.
[http://dx.doi.org/10.1016/j.ijresmar.2006.11.002]

[56]   Dekimpe MG, Geyskens I, Gielens K. Using technology to bring online convenience to offline shopping. Mark Lett 2020; 31(1): 25-9.
[http://dx.doi.org/10.1007/s11002-019-09508-5]

[57]   Tarhini A, Alalwan AA, Al-Qirim N, Algharabat R, Masa'deh R. An analysis of the factors influencing the adoption of online shopping. Int J Technol Diffus 2018; 9(3): 68-87. [IJTD].
[http://dx.doi.org/10.4018/IJTD.2018070105]

[58]   Vlek C, Stallen PJ. Rational and personal aspects of risk. Acta Psychol (Amst) 1980; 45(1-3): 273-300.
[http://dx.doi.org/10.1016/0001-6918(80)90038-4]

[59] McOmish MA, Quester P. Perceived risk and servicescape: The importance of managing the physical evidence in services marketing. In: Proceedings of the 2nd Atelier de Recherche 2005; 39-54.

[60] Hubert M, Blut M, Brock C, Backhaus C, Eberhardt T. Acceptance of smartphone-based mobile shopping: Mobile benefits, customer characteristics, perceived risks, and the impact of application context. Psychol Mark 2017; 34(2): 175-94.
[http://dx.doi.org/10.1002/mar.20982]

[61] Dai B, Forsythe S, Kwon W-S. The impact of online shopping experience on risk perceptions and online purchase intentions: Does product category matter? J Electron Commerce Res 2014; 15(1): 13-24.

[62] Li N, Zhang P. Consumer online shopping attitudes and behavior: An assessment of research. AMCIS 2002 proceedings. 2002; p. 74.

[63] Wu JH, Wang SC. What drives mobile commerce? Inf Manage 2005; 42(5): 719-29.
[http://dx.doi.org/10.1016/j.im.2004.07.001]

[64] Cheong HJ, Mohammed-Baksh S. U.S. consumer m-commerce involvement: Using in-depth interviews to propose an acceptance model of shopping apps-based m-commerce. Cogent Business & Management 2019; 6(1): 1674077.
[http://dx.doi.org/10.1080/23311975.2019.1674077]

[65] Lavery MPJ, Abadi MM, Bauer R, *et al.* Tackling Africa's digital divide. Nat Photonics 2018; 12(5): 249-52.
[http://dx.doi.org/10.1038/s41566-018-0162-z]

[66] Lesakova D. Seniors and their food shopping behavior: An empirical analysis. Procedia Soc Behav Sci 2016; 220: 243-50.
[http://dx.doi.org/10.1016/j.sbspro.2016.05.496]

[67] Ferreira MB. Measuring consumer perceptions of online shopping convenience 2016.

[68] Adadevoh CKMH. Factors that influences the adoption of E-Commerce in the ghanaian banking industry. Int J Innov Res Dev 2018; 7(2): 23-7.
[http://dx.doi.org/10.24940/ijird/2018/v7/i2/FEB18017]

[69] Ewurah SKM. The concept of eGovernment: ICT policy guidelines for the policy makers of Ghana. Journal of Information Security 2017; 8(2): 106-24.
[http://dx.doi.org/10.4236/jis.2017.82008]

[70] Sanou B. Measuring the information society report 2018. Geneva, Switzerland: International Telecommunication Union 2018.

[71] Mensah IK. Overview of e-government adoption and implementation in ghana. *world academy of science, engineering and technology, international science index 109, International Journal of Social, Behavioral, Educational, Economic.* Business and Industrial Engineering 2016; 10(1): 61-72.

[72] Kartiwi M, Hussin H, Suhaimi MA, Mohamed Jalaldeen MR, Amin MR. Impact of external factors on determining E-commerce benefits among SMEs in Malaysia. J Glob Entrep Res 2018; 8(1): 18.
[http://dx.doi.org/10.1186/s40497-018-0105-7]

[73] Mortenson MJ, Vidgen R. A computational literature review of the technology acceptance model. Int J Inf Manage 2016; 36(6): 1248-59.
[http://dx.doi.org/10.1016/j.ijinfomgt.2016.07.007]

[74] Silverman BG, Bachann M, Al-Akharas K. Implications of buyer decision theory for design of e-commerce websites. Int J Hum Comput Stud 2001; 55(5): 815-44.
[http://dx.doi.org/10.1006/ijhc.2001.0500]

[75] TRAN VD. The relationship among product risk, perceived satisfaction and purchase intentions for online shopping. *The Journal of Asian Finance.* Economics and Business 2020; 7(6): 221-31.

[76] Ha NT, Nguyen TLH, Nguyen TPL, Nguye TD. The effect of trust on consumers' online purchase intention: An integration of TAM and TPB. Management Science Letters 2019; 9(9): 1451-60.
[http://dx.doi.org/10.5267/j.msl.2019.5.006]

[77] Celik H. Customer online shopping anxiety within the unified theory of acceptance and use technology (UTAUT) framework. Asia Pac J Mark Log 2016; 28(2).
[http://dx.doi.org/10.1108/APJML-05-2015-0077]

[78] Chiu CM, Wang ETG, Fang YH, Huang HY. Understanding customers' repeat purchase intentions in B2C e-commerce: The roles of utilitarian value, hedonic value and perceived risk. Inf Syst J 2014; 24(1): 85-114.
[http://dx.doi.org/10.1111/j.1365-2575.2012.00407.x]

[79] Al-Debei MM, Akroush MN, Ashouri MI. Consumer attitudes towards online shopping. Internet Res 2015; 25(5): 707-33.
[http://dx.doi.org/10.1108/IntR-05-2014-0146]

[80] Hung SY, Chen CC, Huang NH. An integrative approach to understanding customer satisfaction with e-service of online stores. J Electron Commerce Res 2014; 15(1): 40.

[81] Anesbury Z, Nenycz-Thiel M, Dawes J, Kennedy R. How do shoppers behave online? An observational study of online grocery shopping. J Consum Behav 2016; 15(3): 261-70.
[http://dx.doi.org/10.1002/cb.1566]

[82] Lai PC. Design and Security impact on consumers' intention to use single platform E-payment. Interdiscip Inf Sci 2016; 22(1): 111-22.
[http://dx.doi.org/10.4036/iis.2016.R.05]

[83] Crisp CB, Jarvenpaa SL, Todd PA. Individual differences and internet shopping attitudes and intentions. 1997.

[84] Korgaonkar P, Petrescu M, Becerra E. Shopping orientations and patronage preferences for internet auctions. Int J Retail Distrib Manag 2014; 42(5): 352-68.
[http://dx.doi.org/10.1108/IJRDM-03-2012-0022]

[85] Cho YC, Sagynov E. Exploring factors that affect usefulness, ease of use, trust, and purchase intention in the online environment. International journal of management & information systems 2015; 19(1): 21-36.

[86] Tandon A, Gupta A, Tripathi V. Managing shopping experience through mall attractiveness dimensions. Asia Pac J Mark Log 2016; 28(4): 634-49.
[http://dx.doi.org/10.1108/APJML-08-2015-0127]

[87] Mayer RC, Davis JH, Schoorman FD. An integrative model of organizational trust. Acad Manage Rev 1995; 20(3): 709-34.
[http://dx.doi.org/10.2307/258792]

[88] Suresh AM, Shashikala R. Identifying factors of consumer perceived risk towards online shopping in India. 3rd International Conference on Information and Financial Engineering IPEDR. Vol. 12: 336-41.

[89] Bezes C. Comparing online and in-store risks in multichannel shopping. Int J Retail Distrib Manag 2016; 44(3).
[http://dx.doi.org/10.1108/IJRDM-02-2015-0019]

[90] Alnsour M, Ismael N, Nsoor Z, Feidi M. The perceived risks affecting online shopping adoption in Jordan. Int J Online Mark 2019; 9(2): 1-12. [IJOM].
[http://dx.doi.org/10.4018/IJOM.2019040101]

[91] Gabbiadini A, Greitemeyer T. Uncovering the association between strategy video games and self-regulation: A correlational study. Pers Individ Dif 2017; 104: 129-36.
[http://dx.doi.org/10.1016/j.paid.2016.07.041]

[92] Bettany-Saltikov J, Whittaker VJ. Selecting the most appropriate inferential statistical test for your quantitative research study. J Clin Nurs 2014; 23(11-12): 1520-31.
[http://dx.doi.org/10.1111/jocn.12343] [PMID: 24103052]

[93] Basil M. Survey for formative research. Formative research in social marketing. Singapore: Springer 2017; pp. 251-63.
[http://dx.doi.org/10.1007/978-981-10-1829-9_12]

[94] Walsh E, Brinker JK. Short and sweet? Length and informative content of open-ended responses using SMS as a research mode. J Comput Mediat Commun 2016; 21(1): 87-100.
[http://dx.doi.org/10.1111/jcc4.12146]

[95] Alwin DF. Investigating response errors in survey data. Sociol Methods Res 2014; 43(1): 3-14.
[http://dx.doi.org/10.1177/0049124113507907] [PMID: 26877562]

[96] Middleton A, Bragin E, Morley KI, Parker M. Online questionnaire development: Using film to engage participants and then gather attitudes towards the sharing of genomic data. Soc Sci Res 2014; 44(100): 211-23.
[http://dx.doi.org/10.1016/j.ssresearch.2013.12.004] [PMID: 24468445]

[97] Bryman A, Bell E. Business Research methods. Oxford: Oxford University Press 2015.

[98] Ertürk NO. I Know it, but do I know why? Procedia Soc Behav Sci 2014; 158: 240-6.
[http://dx.doi.org/10.1016/j.sbspro.2014.12.082]

[99] Hom PW, Griffeth RW, Sellaro CL. The validity of Mobley's (1977) model of employee turnover. Organ Behav Hum Perform 1984; 34(2): 141-74.
[http://dx.doi.org/10.1016/0030-5073(84)90001-1] [PMID: 10268421]

[100] Cepeda MS, Fife D, Kihm MA, Mastrogiovanni G, Yuan Y. Comparison of the risks of shopping behavior and opioid abuse between tapentadol and oxycodone and association of shopping behavior and opioid abuse. Clin J Pain 2014; 30(12): 1051-6.
[http://dx.doi.org/10.1097/AJP.0000000000000067] [PMID: 24370606]

[101] Denscombe M. The Good research guide. Maidenhead, England 2014.

[102] Weiss DJ, Dawis RV, England GW. Manual for the Minnesota satisfaction questionnaire. Minnesota studies in vocational rehabilitation 1967.

[103] Green SB, Salkind NJ. Using SPSS for windows and macintosh: Analyzing and understanding data. New Jersey: Pearson 2016.

[104] Jiang LA, Yang Z, Jun M. Measuring consumer perceptions of online shopping convenience. J Serv Manag 2013; 24(2): 191-214.
[http://dx.doi.org/10.1108/09564231311323962]

[105] Shephard A, Pookulangara S, Kinley TR, Josiam BM. Media influence, fashion, and shopping: A gender perspective. J Fash Mark Manag 2016; 20(1): 4-18.
[http://dx.doi.org/10.1108/JFMM-09-2014-0068]

[106] Rehman S, Mohamed R, Ayoup H. The mediating role of organizational capabilities between organizational performance and its determinants. J Glob Entrep Res 2019; 9(1): 30.
[http://dx.doi.org/10.1186/s40497-019-0155-5]

[107] Hair JF, Black WC, Babin BJ, Anderson RE, Tatham R. Multivariate data analysis (7th editio). Harlow: Pearson Education Limited 2010.

[108] Churchill GA Jr. A paradigm for developing better measures of marketing constructs. J Mark Res 1979; 16(1): 64-73.
[http://dx.doi.org/10.1177/002224377901600110]

[109] Cronbach LJ. Coefficient alpha and the internal structure of tests. psychometrika 1951; 16(3): 297-334.

[110] Fornell C, Larcker DF. Structural equation models with unobservable variables and measurement error. Algebra and statistics 1981.

[111] Abed S. An empirical examination of Instagram as an s-commerce channel. Journal of Advances in Management Research 2018; 15(2).

[112] Hangel N, Schmidt-Pfister D. Why do you publish? On the tensions between generating scientific knowledge and publication pressure. Aslib J Inf Manag 2017; 69(5): 529-44.
[http://dx.doi.org/10.1108/AJIM-01-2017-0019]

CHAPTER 3

Digital Transformation of African SMEs: Understanding Digital Transformation

Yomboi Jonas[1,*], Nkayi Kwasi[2], Aloriwor Elijah Kutogichiga[3] and **Felli Gideon Kupule Adobauru[4]**

[1] *St. John's Integrated Senior High/Tech. School – Navrongo, Ghana*

[2] *Tamale Teaching Hospital, Salaga/yendi Rd, Tamale, Ghana*

[3] *Department of Social Studies, Tamale Islamic Science Senior High School, Tamale, Ghana*

[4] *C. K. Tedam University of Technology and Applied Sciences, Navrongo, Ghana*

Abstract: While the current literature has enhanced our understanding of specific aspects of digital transformation, we lack a comprehensive representation of the nature of this transition and the effects it has on SMEs in Africa. Small and medium businesses (SMEs) in Africa are largely responsible for the region's economic growth and development. Digital transformation (DT) of organisations improves resilience; nevertheless, SMEs in Africa have been hesitant to adopt DT due to a number of obstacles. The findings reveal the importance of mobile phones and social media of DT in boosting SMEs in Africa. It has also established digital technology and user experience as the main dimensions of DT.

Keywords: Culture, Challenges, Digital transformation, Digitalisation, Enterprises, Innovation, Information system, Market.

INTRODUCTION

It is widely accepted that Africa's small and medium-sized enterprises (SMEs) play a crucial part in the expansion and development of Africa's economy by, for example, generating new jobs and fostering healthy competition through innovation and the launch of new businesses [1]. SMEs are crucial to the ongoing economic success of both industrialised and developing nations [2, 3]. The Organization for Economic Cooperation and Development (2017) found that a number of nations are struggling due to slow economic development, high unemployment rates, increasing income inequality, and widespread poverty. SMEs contribute significantly to the development of the economy, but they also

---

[*] **Corresponding author Yomboi Jonas:** St. John's Integrated Senior High/Tech. School – Navrongo, Ghana; E-mail: jonasyomboi@gmail.com

Mohammed Majeed, Abdul-Razak Abubakari, Awini Gideon and Jayadatta S. (Eds.)

face growing pressure to address sustainability challenges across economic, environmental, and social aspects [4]. Zambian [5], Nigerian [6], South African [1], Egyptian [7], and Ghanaian scholars have all looked at the impact of the digital revolution on SMEs in Africa [1]. In order to stay competitive, businesses must undertake the challenge and opportunity of digital transformation by digitising current business operations [8]. The competitiveness of businesses and their ability to take advantage of chances for innovation-driven development may be influenced by a number of variables, including those related to the market, to learning, and to the entrepreneurial spirit of the company's leadership [9]. For SMEs to keep their competitive edge over the long term, they need to adopt new technologies and processes of digital manufacturing [10]. Industry as a whole is adopting a variety of distributed data management technologies as part of the cyber-physical system (CPS), and these technologies are being used to allow shifts in the performance of firms' technological and production development, which in turn improves business outcomes [11]. Additionally, digital transformation can be seen as both a driver and a precursor of sustainability, with the latter requiring the former in that industrial firms need to build up enabling digital capabilities to achieve a balanced set of impacts across economic, environmental, and social dimensions [12]. As a result, SMEs may use digital manufacturing techniques to their advantage and pave the route to sustainability in Africa [12 - 14].

New studies have helped us better grasp several facets of the DT phenomena. According to the findings of recent studies, which are in line with the findings of past research on IT-enabled innovation acknowledges that technology is just one part of the intricate complex problem that has to be addressed if companies are to thrive in the digital age. Adjustments to strategy and organization, such as those made to the company's structure, processes, and culture, are required in order to give the opportunity for the establishment of new avenues for the production of value [10]. Despite these advances, a full grasp of this phenomena and its ramifications across all levels of study remains elusive [15, 16].

An increasingly prominent topic in strategic Information System (IS) studies [17], and of interest to practitioners, is digital transformation (DT) [18]. The term "digital transformation" (DT) is used to describe the dramatic changes in society and the economy that have resulted from the advent and proliferation of digital technologies [19 - 21]. According to Fletcher and Griffiths [22], businesses could use the potential of these tools for innovation by creating "strategies that embrace the implications of digital transformation and drive better operational performance".

LITERATURE REVIEW

Small and Medium Enterprises (SMEs)

To be expected, given the diversity of SMEs, the existing literature does not agree on a single, overarching definition. The lack of consensus on a single definition may be traced back to the many different viewpoints on SMEs held by different actors, such as governments, business executives, academics, and politicians. Keskn *et al.* contend, for instance, that different nations define SMEs in different ways, depending on factors like the size of the economy, the number of workers, the amount of sales income, the value of assets, the degree of growth of SMEs, and so on. Many academics argue that SMEs are defined by statute. It is clear from these considerations that a unified definition of SMEs is lacking since all of their facets are difficult to represent in a single formulation. The World Bank lists 32 of the world's 42 poorest nations as being in Africa. Therefore, the World Bank's definition of SMEs is used throughout this article. SMEs are defined as having less than 300 workers, less than US $15.00 million in annual sales or assets, and a loan amount of less than US $1m.

Microbusinesses conducted by a single entrepreneur up to medium-sized companies with dozens of employees are characteristic among Africa's SMEs. In contrast to the medium and large firms, which tend to operate inside the official economy, the vast majority of small businesses are run on the sly. It is estimated that in Africa, 80% of all economic and labour activity takes place in the official and informal sectors. Therefore, SMEs have a considerable impact on the GDP of the area (GDP). In the sub-Saharan African area, SMEs have made important contributions such as those listed below. SMEs account for between 50 and 60 percent of all employment in South Africa and generate 34 percent of the country's gross domestic product (GDP). In Nigeria, SMEs account for an estimated 3 million jobs every year. SMEs contribute between 38% and 60% to the economies of Kenya, Ghana, Cameroon, Rwanda, and Zambia, respectively. According to these numbers, SMEs are crucial to Africa's economic and social progress.

SMEs cover a wide spectrum, from micro-firms maintained by only one or two people with little or no growth to large corporations with hundreds of workers [6]. There is a wide range of enterprises, from those that need little capital to launch to those that need millions [23, 24]. Various industries and regions of the globe use various metrics, such as staff count, total assets, yearly revenue, and capital investments, to define SMEs [25]. Various studies have shown how difficult it is to agree on a single definition of SMEs. Research conducted by Auciello (1975) in 75 different nations revealed that the target countries really employed more than 75 different definitions. This shows convincingly that there is no universally agreed-upon definition of SMEs. Definitions will continue to change depending on factors such as geographic location, kind of business, company size, assets, and goods. In the United States and Canada, for instance, SMEs are defined as having less than 500 people, whereas enterprises with fewer than 100 employees and revenues are considered "small." In Germany, SMEs are defined as those with less than 250 workers; in Belgium, this number drops to 100. There is a cap of 250 workers for a SME in Germany, but only 100 for a similar entity in Belgium [2]. In Africa and other developing regions, a firm with 100 or more workers is considered big, whereas one with less than five is considered tiny. In the United States and other industrialised nations, a company with 500 to 499 workers is considered to be of medium size [26]. Most common definitions are quantitative in nature, emphasizing on things like size, revenue, and the number of people employed by a company. Although extremely small firms may have less than 50 employees and micro-enterprises have between 5 and 10 employees, the most current acknowledged definition from several studies defines SMEs as those with fewer than 250 employees. In addition, it is clear that in low and lower middle-income nations, over half of enterprises have less than 100 workers [2, 5, 7, 16, 26, 27 - 29].

Digital Transformation

Definitions of the digital transformation, often known as "digitalization," are uncommon in current writings. According to our research, the digital transformation has been variously characterised as a cultural shift [18, 30 - 33] and a social phenomenon [17, 34] and, for businesses, as the development or modification of a business model [35, 36]

The so-called "digital" generations [8, 29, 35 - 37] are largely responsible for this shift in perspective, since digital technology permeates every aspect of their lives. Companies in this environment need the flexibility to either modify their current business model or create a whole new one.

The digital transformation of firms as a business model, however, appears problematic and incomplete since it might alter other parts of a company, including its culture, organisational structure, workspaces, and ethics. We offer the following definition of digital transformation: "a process of change, either revolutionary or evolutionary." Adopting and using digital technology is the first step toward an implicit or intentional comprehensive change in a company with the goal of value generation.

The Dimensions of Digital Transformation

Based on our analysis of the available literature, we can identify two key dimensions: (1) digital technology, and (2) user experience.

Digital Technologies

As its name indicates, digital transformation is essentially a transition that has resulted from the development of new technological capabilities. There also exist internet technologies [8, 9, 16, 22, 25, 29, 38 - 41] and analytical technologies [42]. These three overlapping and complimentary technologies have really advanced over the course of the last several years, mostly as a result of developments in cloud computing.

User Experience

Users are now at front and centre in business strategy thanks to the digital transformation. There has been a steady rise in customers' expectations for a superior level of quality in everything they purchase. They count on businesses to be flexible and cater to their own requirements. This is especially true of the "digital" generation of today [43], who are fluent in the latest technological advances and have a significant knack for imparting their knowledge to others through social media [18, 25, 44 - 46]. Companies need to adjust how they talk about their goods and services to match the shifting tastes of their customers. Therefore, the marketing department is often the first to undergo change as a result of digitalization. The latter is achieved, in particular, *via* the use of CRM (Customer Relationship Management) solutions of the most recent generation that include a robust social component through the social networks analysis modules.

Internal users, such as collaborators or workers, are also a part of the user experience and should be considered [24, 47]. In many cases, companies lag behind the competition because their staff are already adopting cutting-edge technology in their personal lives. The widespread use of remote work, in particular, is a direct result of the availability of mobile and collaborative technology, which have altered workplaces and altered traditional methods of work. In order to increase the quality and productivity of their workers' work, businesses are investing in mobility, linked items, and collaboration platforms. Along with digitising HR processes, ERM (Employee Relationship Management) software was introduced. Tools of this kind treat employees as an organization's internal customers and strive to provide them with excellent service.

Digital Transformation Tools SMEs Use

There is no denying of the importance of social media, mobile phones, and analytics in today's business world, particularly when it comes to reaching out to potential and existing clients for their use of digital tools [48]. Customers often check these online venues for information about new products and promotions. Keep in mind that SA has more than six billion mobile phones and that Facebook alone has more than a billion members [49, 50]. In addition, when businesses reach a certain level of development along the "digital intensity dimension," they become more effective at generating income from their existing assets [51].

Moreover, digital transformation streamlines the procedure of connecting the company with its internal and external stakeholders, including customers, partners, suppliers, *etc* [13]. In addition, busy company owners will have the ability to initiate and oversee the operation of many enterprises at once. The advent of digital transformation has the potential to significantly enhance several economic qualities conducive to corporate expansion [52]. In addition, the proliferation of customer-facing devices and distribution channels made possible by digital transformation encourages widespread content adoption [12].

Business value is molded by digital transformation's facilitation of innovative methods, enhanced designs, and new ways of operation [2]. Those businesses that successfully adopt digital transformation will benefit from the advantages it brings. It may occur in any of three ways: enhanced interaction with and satisfaction for customers; optimised internal processes; or the introduction of new business models [53]. Similar to how digital transformation boosts corporate innovation compared to rivals [54], SMEs are pushed to implement suitable internet technology in order to enhance their internal procedures, therefore enhancing their product *via* more rapid contact with clients and more effective marketing and distribution [2]. Therefore, customer service may be improved greatly with the implementation of digital transformation.

Effect of DT on SMEs

Different companies may feel different effects of digital transformation [48]. The effects of digital transformation on various industry topics may vary. According to Fletcher and Griffiths [22], for instance, sectors with well-established business-to-consumer (B2C) ties and a customer-centric emphasis may be impacted by digital transformation sooner and more profoundly than those with a primarily business-to-business (B2B) orientation. Ismail *et al.* [26], argue that thanks to digitalization, SMEs now have a better chance of getting off the ground and competing successfully in the global market. Rapid product or service innovation, decreased product life cycles, and cross-sector disruption are all results of digital transformation, necessitating new configurations of company strategies [20]. Even though digital transformation uses digital technologies and capabilities to affect many parts of the business operation to produce value, it is crucial to understand how this affects the business component to ensure its effective implementation [52].

There is currently an increasing amount of pressure on businesses with dispersed branches to undergo a digital transformation of their operations. For instance, if they don't want to fall behind more innovative and sophisticated rivals and other market participants, they need to make necessary changes quickly [18]. Lutfi *et al.* [11], argued that SMEs in Africa are better equipped to achieve sustainable development when they use new technology. From a technical standpoint, sophisticated technologies like social media and big data play a central role in business model innovation (BMI) for most enterprises, and hence for SMEs [33]. Similar to how BE, processes, business models, products, and connections are impacted by digital transformation to increase an enterprise's size and performance, Lutfi *et al.* [11], noted that these factors are also referenced in the context of digital transformation. In addition, digitalization provides an opportunity to meet the needs of present customers for highly flexible supply and demand for unique items.

DISCUSSION

This section discusses digital transformation strategies and the business operations of SMEs to improve resilience. The use of digital technology in SME company operations has the ability to alter SME operations and boost their competitiveness. SMEs must be more malleable in order to survive in today's uncertain economic climate. When competing in a market where conditions are constantly shifting, SMEs must be able to adapt fast. The two are related in a way that is affected by the specifics of the business climate in which SMEs function. These relationships determine whether or not SMEs can establish the long-term resilience necessary to compete in the global market.

In order to achieve the resilience pillars, SMEs need to change their company processes, organisational culture, and structures using process and human resource management. Africa's SMEs may make use of digital technology to increase their market reach, diversify their supply chain, and accept digital payments and marketing campaigns. All of these things could help in some manner with competitiveness and finding new sources of income and value. To do so, SMEs need a plan for incorporating digital technologies that provide quantifiable advantages. Thus, an adoption plan should take into account the contextual elements stated in the results section that need to be addressed to establish an enabling corporate environment.

A situation awareness approach is necessary for achieving digitally enabled resilience *via* the process management component. African SMEs may be well-equipped to handle the issues unique to their environments and make strategic choices about how to respond. For instance, if SMEs had access to up-to-th e-minute data about, say, shifting consumer expectations or technological development, they could respond swiftly. Preparation may be made by small and medium-sized businesses by analysing and managing their primary vulnerabilities and adaptive capability. The importance and usefulness of a technique like situational awareness depend on the specific circumstances in which it is used. It follows that it is crucial for African SMEs to understand the importance of digital technologies to their operations and how such technologies might help them achieve their goals. The study's authors suggest that responsiveness, a cornerstone of organisational resilience, is fostered by adopting a situation awareness approach. As a business tactic, situational awareness may help SMEs in the African environment identify and pursue untapped possibilities.

SMEs may ease into the incorporation of digital technology by developing a third strategy: the identification and management of significant weaknesses in their operations. To do so, they must have a firm grasp of the operational and managerial pillars upon which their enterprises rest, as well as the ways in which digital technology might facilitate these pillars' activities. Digital efforts like mobile or digital wallets, for instance, have revolutionised financial services and enabled new payment patterns for SMEs. As a result, it is crucial for SMEs to understand how such an endeavour may affect their daily operations. The owners and workers of SMEs, for instance, need to be well-versed in data privacy and cybercrime problems. The use of digital tools and social media makes these problems much more complex, making it all the more important for SMEs in the African environment to recognise and address the threats they pose.

Digital efforts may also include training for employees who will utilise the new tools to advance the company. SMEs should evaluate their adaptability in light of their knowledge of their operating surroundings and their vulnerabilities. SMEs have a better chance of surviving in the long run if they adopt a strategy that incorporates digital technology, managerial best practices, market knowledge, and agility.

CONCLUSION

In the African context, SMEs are seen as the engine that drives the continent's economy. However, most SMEs either cease to exist or collapse within their first two years. According to the available literature, the failure of many small and medium-sized enterprises (SMEs) digital efforts is attributable to their leaders' failure to make the connection between digital technology and the sources of revenue generation. This article set out to determine how SMEs in the African setting may create all-encompassing plans for using digital technology in their business processes in order to strengthen their resilience and enhance their profit generators. This, according to the study's authors, is because few SMEs have adopted methods designed to help them make the most of the digital tools at their disposal. According to the study's authors, SMEs may create a climate conducive to the flexibility, responsiveness, and change inherent in their operations by formulating overarching plans.

Business process reengineering is a crucial part of the digital transformation process. Accordingly, it is both socially and culturally produced, with traditions and cultures simultaneously impacting both its perception and implementation. This calls for all-encompassing policies to help SMEs take advantage of the revolutionary potential of digital technology. Many SMEs in the African market have difficulties in their endeavours due to geographical limits. Understanding the operational environment completely is essential for developing strategies for integrating technology. According to the analysed literature, the socio-technical and economic contexts are both important and interrelated. Because of these external constraints, SMEs are hampered in their attempts to embrace and use digital technology and build digitally-enabled resilience in order to participate in the global digital economy.

REFERENCES

[1] Kraus S, Jones P, Kailer N, Weinmann A, Chaparro-Banegas N, Roig-Tierno N. Digital transformation: An overview of the current state of the art of research. *Journals.Sagepub.* SAGE Open 2021; 11(3).
[http://dx.doi.org/10.1177/21582440211047576]

[2] Schwertner K. Digital transformation. 2015.
[http://dx.doi.org/10.15547/tjs.2017.s.01.065]

[3] Bai C, Quayson M, Sarkis J. COVID-19 pandemic digitization lessons for sustainable development of micro-and small- enterprises. In Sustainable Production and Consumption. 2021; 27: p. 1989.
[http://dx.doi.org/10.1016/j.spc.2021.04.035]

[4] Teichert R. Digital transformation maturity: A systematic review of literature. Acta Univ Agric Silvic Mendel Brun 2019; 67(6): 1673-87.
[http://dx.doi.org/10.11118/actaun201967061673]

[5] Mergel I, Edelmann N, Haug N. Defining digital transformation: Results from expert interviews. Gov Inf Q 2019; 36(4): 101385.
[http://dx.doi.org/10.1016/j.giq.2019.06.002]

[6] Andriole SJ. Five myths about digital transformation. MIT Sloan Manag Rev 2018; 58(3): 13-8.
[http://dx.doi.org/10.7551/mitpress/11633.003.0005]

[7] Ebert C, Duarte CHC. Digital transformation. IEEE Softw 2018; 35(4): 16-21.

[http://dx.doi.org/10.1109/MS.2018.2801537]

[8] Westerman G, Bonnet D. Revamping your business through digital transformation. MIT Sloan Manag Rev 2015; 56(3): 2-5.

[9] Morakanyane R, Grace A. eConference, P. O.-B., & 2017, undefined. (2017). Conceptualizing Digital Transformation in Business Organizations: A Systematic Review of Literature. AiselAisnetOrg 2017.
[http://dx.doi.org/10.18690/978-961-286-043-1.30]

[10] Jeza S, Mpele Lekhanya L. The influence of digital transformation on the growth of small and medium enterprises in South Africa. Probl Perspect Manag 2022; 20(3): 297-309.
[http://dx.doi.org/10.21511/ppm.20(3).2022.24]

[11] Lee CH, Liu CL, Trappey AJC, Mo JPT, Desouza KC. Understanding digital transformation in advanced manufacturing and engineering: A bibliometric analysis, topic modeling and research trend discovery. Adv Eng Inform 2021; 50: 101428.
[http://dx.doi.org/10.1016/j.aei.2021.101428]

[12] Verhoef PC, Broekhuizen T, Bart Y, *et al.* Digital transformation: A multidisciplinary reflection and research agenda. J Bus Res 2021; 122: 889-901.
[http://dx.doi.org/10.1016/j.jbusres.2019.09.022]

[13] Chanias S, Hess T. Understanding digital transformation strategy formation: Insights from Europe's automotive industry. Pacific Asia Conference on Information Systems, PACIS 2016 - Proceedings 2016. https://www.researchgate.net/profile/Thomas-Hess-6/publication/311443349_Understanding_Digital_Transformation_Strategy_Formation_Insights_from_Europe's_Automotive_Industry/links/5c310fe2458515a4c7109a03/Understanding-Digital-Transformation-Strategy-Format

[14] Maijanen P. Managing digital transformation. In Media Management Matters. 2020; pp. 204-17.
[http://dx.doi.org/10.4324/9780429265396-13]

[15] Bowers B J. Grounded theory. NLN Publications 1988; 33-59.
[http://dx.doi.org/10.1177/1609406915618324]

[16] Guillén MF, Cartwright PA, Yip GS. The digital transformation of traditional businesses. MIT Sloan Manag Rev 2021; 44(4): 31-48.
[http://dx.doi.org/10.2307/j.ctv2hdrfxp.6]

[17] Sebastian I I M, Ross J J W, *et al.* C. B.-S. information, 2020, undefined, Moloney, K. G., Ross, J. J. W., Fonstad, N. O., Beath, C., & Mocker, M. How big old companies navigate digital transformation 2020; 16(3): 197-213.

[18] Nadkarni S, Prügl R. Digital transformation: A review, synthesis and opportunities for future research. Management Review Quarterly 2021; 71(2): 233-341.
[http://dx.doi.org/10.1007/s11301-020-00185-7]

[19] Karmous-Edwards G, Tomic S, Cooper JP. Developing a unified definition of digital twins. In Journal - American Water Works Association 2022; 114(6): 76-8.
[http://dx.doi.org/10.1002/awwa.1946]

[20] Zapata ML, Berrah L, Tabourot L. Is a digital transformation framework enough for manufacturing smart products? The case of Small and Medium Enterprises. Procedia Manuf 2020; 42: 70-5.
[http://dx.doi.org/10.1016/j.promfg.2020.02.024]

[21] Šimberová I, Korauš A, Schüller D, Smolíková L, Straková J, Váchal J. Threats and Opportunities in Digital Transformation in SMEs from the Perspective of Sustainability: A Case Study in the Czech Republic. Sustainability 2022; 14(6): 3628.
[http://dx.doi.org/10.3390/su14063628]

[22] Vial G. Understanding digital transformation. Managing Digital Transformation 2021; 13-66.

[23] Wynn M, Olayinka O. E-business strategy in developing countries: A framework and checklist for the small business sector. Sustainability 2021; 13(13): 7356.

[http://dx.doi.org/10.3390/su13137356]

[24] Fletcher G, Griffiths M. Digital transformation during a lockdown. Int J Inf Manage 2020; 55: 102185.
[http://dx.doi.org/10.1016/j.ijinfomgt.2020.102185] [PMID: 32836642]

[25] Hitchen EL, Nylund PA, Ferràs X, Mussons S. Social media: Open innovation in SMEs finds new support. J Bus Strategy 2017; 38(3): 21-9.https://www.emerald.com/insight/content/doi/10.1108/jbs-02-2016-0015/full/html
[http://dx.doi.org/10.1108/JBS-02-2016-0015]

[26] Stark J. Digital transformation of industry: Continuing Change. 2020. Available from: Available from: https://link.springer.com/content/pdf/10.1007/978-3-030-41001-8.pdf.

[27] Berman SJ. Digital transformation: Opportunities to create new business models. Strategy Leadersh 2012; 40(2): 16-24.
[http://dx.doi.org/10.1108/10878571211209314]

[28] Matt C, Hess T, Benlian A. Digital transformation strategies. In Business and Information Systems Engineering. 2015; 57: pp. (5)339-43.
[http://dx.doi.org/10.1007/s12599-015-0401-5]

[29] Maisiri W, van Dyk L. Industry 4.0 readiness assessment for South African industries. S Afr J Ind Eng 2019; 30(3): 134-48.
[http://dx.doi.org/10.7166/30-3-2231]

[30] Sousa MJ, Rocha Á. Digital learning: Developing skills for digital transformation of organizations. Future Gener Comput Syst 2019; 91: 327-34.
[http://dx.doi.org/10.1016/j.future.2018.08.048]

[31] Commission A U. Digital transformation for youth employment and Agenda 2063 in Central Africa 2021.
[http://dx.doi.org/10.1787/f2e7ffb6-en]

[32] Tolstolesova L, Glukhikh I, Yumanova N, Arzikulov O. Digital transformation of public-private partnership tools. Journal of Risk and Financial Management 2021; 14(3): 121.
[http://dx.doi.org/10.3390/jrfm14030121]

[33] KPMG. Currents of change: The KPMG Survey of Corporate Responsibility Reporting 2015. KPMG Corporate Responsibility Reporting, 2015; 1-48. https://assets.kpmg.com/content/dam/kpmg/pdf/2016/02/kpmg-international-survey-of-corporate-responsibility-reporting-2015.pdf

[34] Danielsen F, Flak LS, Sæbø Ø. Understanding digital transformation in government.Public Administration and Information Technology. Springer 2022; Vol. 38: pp. 151-87.
[http://dx.doi.org/10.1007/978-3-030-92945-9_7]

[35] Ziółkowska M J, Zawadzka D, Pérez A. Digital transformation and marketing activities in small and medium-sized enterprises. MdpiCom 2021; 13(5): 2512.
[http://dx.doi.org/10.3390/su13052512]

[36] van Veldhoven Z, Vanthienen J. Designing a comprehensive understanding of digital transformation and its impact. 32nd Bled EConference Humanizing Technology for a Sustainable Society, BLED 2019 - Conference Proceedings 2020; 745-63.
[http://dx.doi.org/10.18690/978-961-286-280-0.39]

[37] Henriette E, Feki M, Boughzala I. The shape of digital transformation: A systematic literature review. Mediterranean Conference on Information Systems (MCIS) Proceedings 2015; 1-13.https://aisel.aisnet.org/mcis2015/10/

[38] Kretzschmar M. A Roadmap to support SMEs in the SADC Region to Prepare for Digital Transformation by 2021; 1-239.http://scholar.sun.ac.za/handle/10019.1/109836

[39] Mahamat MF, Gurría Á. 2021), de AU/OECD. AUC, Addis Ababa/OECD Paris Emprendimiento y Negocios Internacionales,. 2021; pp. 26-9.

[http://dx.doi.org/10.20420/eni.2021.427]

[40]   Lanzolla G, Anderson J. Digital transformation. Bus Strateg Rev 2008; 19(2): 72-6.
        [http://dx.doi.org/10.1111/j.1467-8616.2008.00539.x]

[41]   Tabrizi B, Lam E. review, K. G.-H. business, & 2019, undefined. (2019). Digital transformation is not
        about technology. 2019. Available from: https://bluecirclemarketing.com/wp-content/uploads/
        2019/07/Digital-Transformation-Is-Not-About-Technology.pdf

[42]   Digital transformation: A literature review and guidelines for future research. 745 Advances in
        Intelligent Systems and Computing 411 2018; 411-21.
        [http://dx.doi.org/10.1007/978-3-319-77703-0_41]

[43]   Kamanga R, Alexandra PM. Facilitated adoption of accounting information systems: A first step to
        digital transformation in township microenterprises. 2019 Open Innovations Conference, OI 2019
        2019; 312-9.
        [http://dx.doi.org/10.1109/OI.2019.8908236]

[44]   Sandada M, Pooe D, Dhurup M. Strategic planning and its relationship with business performance
        among small and medium enterprises in south africa. Int Bus Econ Res J 2014; 13(3): 659. [IBER].
        [http://dx.doi.org/10.19030/iber.v13i3.8602]

[45]   Rambaruth A, Khatoon Adam J, Babu Naidu Krishna S. Strategic Management in Construction Firms
        with Focus on Small and Medium Enterprises: a Case Study eThekwini, South Africa In Construction
        Business & Project Management 2021; 1-11. https://journals.uct.ac.za/index.php/jcbm/
        article/view/1235

[46]   Nambisan S, Wright M, Feldman M. The digital transformation of innovation and entrepreneurship:
        Progress, challenges and key themes. Res Policy 2019; 48(8): 103773.
        [http://dx.doi.org/10.1016/j.respol.2019.03.018]

[47]   Ziyadin S, Suieubayeva S, Utegenova A. Digital transformation in business. Lecture Notes in
        Networks and Systems. Springer 2020; Vol. 84: pp. 408-15.
        [http://dx.doi.org/10.1007/978-3-030-27015-5_49]

[48]   Matt DT, Rauch E. SME 4.0: The role of small-and medium-sized enterprises in the digital
        transformation. In Industry 40 for SMEs: Challenges, Opportunities and Requirements. 2020; pp. 3-36.
        [http://dx.doi.org/10.1007/978-3-030-25425-4_1]

[49]   Llopis-Albert C, Rubio F, Valero F. Impact of digital transformation on the automotive industry.
        Technol Forecast Soc Change 2021; 162: 120343.
        [http://dx.doi.org/10.1016/j.techfore.2020.120343] [PMID: 33052150]

[50]   Lutfi A, Alsyouf A, Almaiah M A, et al. Factors Influencing the Adoption of Big Data Analytics in the
        Digital Transformation Era: Case Study of Jordanian SMEs. MdpiCom 2022; 14(3): 1802.
        [http://dx.doi.org/10.3390/su14031802]

[51]   Cant MC, Wiid JA. The use of traditional marketing tools by SMEs in an emerging economy: A South
        African perspective. Probl Perspect Manag 2016; 14(1): 64-70.
        [http://dx.doi.org/10.21511/ppm.14(1).2016.07]

[52]   Westerman G, Bonnet D, Mcafee A. The nine elements of digital transformation opinion & analysis.
        MIT Sloan Manag Rev 2014; 55(3): 1-6.

[53]   Ismail R, Jeffery R, Belle JP. Using ICT as a Value Adding Tool in South African SMEs. Journal of
        African Research in Business & Technology 2011; 2011: 1-12.
        [http://dx.doi.org/10.5171/2011.470652]

[54]   Schallmo DRA, Williams CA. History of digital transformation. In Springer. 2018; pp. 3-8.
        [http://dx.doi.org/10.1007/978-3-319-72844-5_2]

CHAPTER 4

An Insight into the Consequences of Digitalization and Digital Technologies for Small and Medium Enterprises (SMEs) in Africa

Jayadatta S.[1,*] and **Mohammed Majeed**[2]

[1] *KLE's Institute of Management Studies (IMSR), Hubballi, Karnataka 580031, India*

[2] *Department of Marketing, Tamale Technical University, Tamale-Ghana*

Abstract: IMF (2020) estimates that 20 million jobs must be created annually in SSA and Africa at large to accommodate the region's expanding labor force. However, digital technologies like email, the internet, and mobile money have a huge potential to generate wealth and jobs that African businesses still need to realize. Even though mobile phone technology has helped spread Internet-based innovations throughout the region, this process is slowed down by a vast Internet divide; businesses and people use these technologies less than they could. In 2015, Internet penetration rates in African nations were below 60% of the total population, with penetration rates as low as 5% in some nations including Niger, Sierra Leone, and Guinea-Bissau. Again in 2015, small African firms employed almost 80% of the labor force on the continent. But surveys by the World Bank between 2013 and 2018 show that less than 60% of SMEs used email for business, and less than 30% used websites for the same thing. In contrast, 90% of major businesses polled within the same time period acknowledged utilizing email and/or a website for conducting business. Since SMEs are currently the largest employers and wealth creators in the region, the poor dissemination and adoption of digital technology severely limit their ability to advance. More specifically, and unlike previous research-based analyses of the digitalization of African firms, the research article combines quantitative analysis and qualitative data to give readers a bird's-eye view of how digital technologies affect the performance of small and medium-sized enterprises (SMEs) in Africa and the opportunities for private sector growth that come with the ongoing digitalization of the economy.

Keywords: Digital technologies, Internet-based innovations, Sdoption of digital technology, Sub-Saharan Africa.

* **Corresponding author Jayadatta S.:** KLE's Institute of Management Studies (IMSR), Hubballi, Karnataka 580031, India; E-mail: Jayadattaster@gmail.com

Mohammed Majeed, Abdul-Razak Abubakari, Awini Gideon and Jayadatta S. (Eds.)

INTRODUCTION

The use and spread of digital technology will likely determine Africa's prosperity in the future. Where people and businesses are severely constrained in their daily interactions by high levels of uncertainty, a lack of infrastructure, high transaction costs, and informational asymmetries, digital technologies play a critical role. The COVID-19 issue has highlighted these market imperfections, which are frequently structural in Africa. According to the Union (2020), Africa needs to add over 20 million jobs annually to accommodate the continent's growing labor force. However, digital technologies like email, the internet, and mobile money have a huge potential to generate wealth and jobs that African businesses still need to fully realize. Despite the fact that mobile phone technology has aided in the spread of Internet-based innovations throughout the region, this dynamic requires improvement due to a wide Internet divide and low adoption of these technologies among businesses and individuals. In 2015, Internet penetration rates in African nations were below 60% of the total population, with penetration rates as low as 5% in some nations including Niger, Sierra Leone, and Guinea-Bissau. Again in 2015, small African firms employed almost 80% of the labor force on the continent [1]. Yet, according to World Bank Enterprise Surveys conducted between 2013 and 2018, less than 60% of SMEs utilized email for business activities, and less than 30% utilized websites for similar purposes. In contrast, 90% of major businesses polled within the same time period acknowledged utilizing email and/or a website for conducting business. Since SMEs are currently the largest employers and wealth creators in the region, the poor dissemination and adoption of digital technology severely limits their ability to advance. Expanding digital technologies like mobile money are frequently referred to as "leapfrogging technologies" in Africa. According to the leapfrogging theory [2], technical advancements have a direct impact on how nations' fortunes change on a global scale. According to this idea, in the event of significant technical advancement, an "advanced" nation's reliance on legacy systems may render newer technologies less desirable in the short term due to their lower profitability, delaying their adoption. Compared to countries that are behind in old technology, are less wealthy, and pay their workers less, they are much more likely to want to give up on the old technology and switch to the new, which is much more profitable from their point of view. Lagging nations that adopt new technologies see increases in productivity, employment, and production in the industries that use those technologies. In industries with a high technological content, the nations that had previously lagged now lead. Could Sub-Saharan Africa (SSA) experience a "reversal of fortune" as a result of digital technologies? It seems relevant to consider mobile-based technologies as having significant leapfrogging potential in Africa's imperfect markets and underdeveloped infrastructure. However, it is still too early to declare a digital-induced growth miracle in the continent [3]. Many obstacles must be overcome if African countries are to break free from the under-industrialization trap, they have found themselves in and promote job creation and economic transformations through digitally enhanced connections and depth. Despite these problems, the leapfrogging theory gives some ideas about how the growth of the digital economy could help Africa move forward. On the one hand, the continent's connection to the world's high-speed Internet through the installation of high-capacity submarine telecommunication cables [4] has made the mobile phone a standard tool for making cheaper communications, including Internet communications [5, 6]. A group of mobile phone companies called the GSMA says that by 2020, more than 700 million smartphone connections will be in Africa. This figure is more than double that expected in North America and very close to that in Europe. Digital technologies can first help a corporation's internal processes. The penetration of digital technologies, such as computer and mobile technologies applications, such as email, websites, spreadsheet software, social networks, and digital platforms, has altered the organization's organizational structure, production processes, communication protocols, and other aspects. This has also helped the firm create its own digital knowledge. This results in improved input usage and innovation processes, fluidized communication and coordination between company employees, easier access to crucial information for decision-making, and operations expansion into new markets [5, 7, 8]. This is especially true for Internet-related technology, which not only increases a company's input use and innovation efficiency but also makes it much easier to gather data on administrative procedures (like business licenses), market and political risks, the structure of the tax system, tariffs and non-tariff measures, customer and competitor profiles, and other topics. It is interesting to note that these benefits are probably crucial for the Small and Medium Enterprises (SMEs) that are the subject of this report because they might be better able to adopt these technologies because of more adaptable organizational and management practices [9, 10]. Various revolutions in the structure of organizations, industries, and socioeconomic interactions have resulted from the diffusion of digital technologies within and among firms [11]. Fundamental digital tools like email, websites, and mobile money, as well as more advanced tools like blockchain technology, cloud computing, and artificial intelligence, can unleash the growth potential of African businesses primarily because of their ability to enhance internal operations and address market and governmental failures. Adopting digital technology provides benefits for enterprises as a whole, and there are also potential indirect consequences on business performance as a result of various spillovers anticipated from its deployment. The private sector's adoption of these technologies may further polarize the labor market and exacerbate economic inequality because the individual and spillover effects of the adoption and diffusion of digital technologies are likely to be heterogeneous among businesses and workers.

First, the internal operations of a corporation can benefit from digital technologies. The firm's organizational structure, production processes, communication protocols, and other aspects have changed because of the widespread use of computers and mobile devices and their associated software like email, internet, spreadsheet software, social media, and other digital platforms, to name a few. This has also helped the firm create its own digital knowledge. This improves the use of input and innovation processes, makes it easier for employees to work together and talk to each other, and makes it easier to get to important information for making decisions [1, 7]. It also makes it possible for operations to grow into new markets. This is especially true for Internet-related technology, which not only improves a company's input use and innovation efficiency but also makes it much simpler to collect data on various topics, such as regulatory procedures (such as obtaining a business license), market and political risks, tax system design, tariffs and non-tariff measures, customer and rival profiles, and many others. It's interesting to note that these benefits are probably important for the Small and Medium Enterprises (SMEs) that are the subject of this report because they might be better able to adopt these technologies because of more adaptable organizational and management practices [9, 10]. However, smaller African businesses may not be able to afford Internet technologies due to their high costs. Mobile phone technologies, especially mobile money, on the other hand, have become very popular among small businesses, especially in Africa, because they are inexpensive and easy to use [12]. Microenterprise performance, particularly productivity in low-income countries, has been found to be improved by reduced information search and other transaction costs as well as improved risk-sharing [1, 3, 13, 14]. Mobile money is a unique innovation in digital finance that goes beyond the use of mobile phones as ICT. Academics and NGOs alike have taken notice, and it's been great for Africa's micro- and small-scale enterprises [4, 12, 15]. Businesses can use mobile money, which is a form of electronic currency, to make payments such as utility bills, taxes, employee salaries, and social transfers *via* text message (SMS) even when they don't have access to the Internet. Financial institutions in Africa often exclude smaller businesses. As a result of numerous market imperfections, which are typical in many African economies, and the high transaction costs and informational asymmetries that have prevented the traditional banking sector from taking them into account, these issues have been largely ignored [2, 12, 16]. However, there is a growing body of research examining how mobile money affects (small) businesses that operate in non-agricultural areas. The few studies examining how mobile money use affects businesses highlight the advantages of this technology for investment, labor market results, access to financing, and innovation [2, 10]. Depending on how strategic these technologies are for the operations of the organization, adoption of more advanced digital technologies may also be particularly beneficial to a firm's productivity and expansion prospects. For instance, adopting a website may enable businesses to spend less time and money engaging with partners, increasing sales and overseas market shares. Businesses and governments in fields like healthcare, education, and digital financial services stand to benefit greatly from blockchain technology due to the decentralized, transparent, and encrypted nature of the information communicated through this technology [4, 6]. Cloud computing, big data, and artificial intelligence (AI) are additional emerging digital technologies that have the potential to help businesses advance by transforming their decision-making procedures in settings with limited access to and high-quality information [10]. Second, through enhancing the corporate environment, digital technology may also contribute to improved company performance and employment generation. Aker [12] and Aker and Fafchamps [13] say that essential Internet technologies can help business operations by making it easier to use formal financial services, reducing price variation, and making it easier to use essential public services (1, 5]. A company's ability to communicate with its customers and suppliers, interact with the government and bureaucracy, even out any informational imbalances, and reduce the costs associated with the financial and non-financial aspects of its bilateral transactions are all enhanced by the use of email. Owning a website may help businesses position themselves better in the market and along the global value chain without the need for pre-existing business ties [9, 15], which lowers the cost of communication and information search to find clients and suppliers. Similar to this, more advanced technologies like online marketplaces and employment platforms are needed to improve market functionality by connecting suppliers and customers at a low cost. These anticipated systemic consequences of digital technologies imply the possibility of spillovers from their adoption by private companies.

Digital Spillovers

Digital spillovers, also called externalities, are the unintended benefits or costs that come from the spread of digital technologies and knowledge outside the company. They are caused by the network goods and general-purpose nature of digital technologies [4, 6, 12, 15], which can be used in all parts of an economy and whose benefits grow with the size of a user's network [11]. For instance, the rise of digital job platforms like Lynk in Kenya helps both formal and informal workers find jobs and improves the distribution of workers in different places and industries. In West Africa, e-commerce companies like Jumia help local shops and artisans reach more customers. Simpler technologies like email, websites, and mobile money are spreading outside of businesses. This speeds up and simplifies economic transactions between businesses and industries, making it easier for them to get access to capital and expertise, but it also makes competition fiercer and causes structural change. Therefore, the spread of digital technology might be predicted to have both positive and negative externalities. Sharing knowledge, best practices, procedures, and innovations connected to digital technologies leads to positive digital knowledge spillovers [6, 7, 8]. According to Marsh *et al.* [11], there are two types of digital knowledge spillovers: (within) industry spillovers, which are knowledge originating from competitors, and cross- or inter-industry spillovers, which are knowledge created from outside the industry. The second type of knowledge spillover is less well understood. It says that knowledge is made and spread across industries, such as when industries upstream and downstream talk to each other and share ideas, methods, practices, and so on. Both theoretical and empirical research has focused much attention on the first type of information spillover [5, 7, 8]. Gorg & Greenaway [6] claim that rivalry, imitation behavior, and skill gain are the three drivers that drive technical knowledge spillovers. Imitation refers to non-adopters or less effective technology adopters integrating technologies and related processes into their industrial function. The generation and/or transfer of digital knowledge that is made possible by worker flow between firms in a particular region or sector is related to the acquisition of skills. In terms of competition, firms that adopt new technologies may face additional pressure to adopt those technologies or to employ them more effectively. Each mechanism is connected to the others since, in a highly competitive context; acquiring employees with excellent digital abilities may lead to the imitation mechanism, for example. When other businesses employ similar digital technologies more often, there may be negative digital spillovers that result in higher rivalry and revenue loss for businesses with low technology absorption capacity (Görg & Greenaway, 2004; [11]). If first-movers or dominant companies use digital technology faster and more efficiently, or if their biggest and best-equipped competitors do the same, it could slow or even stop other companies from leaving domestic or foreign markets. This limited capacity to absorb can be explained by the slow adoption of promising digital technologies within industries, the lack of exposure to global competition, the lack of digital skills within the firm, the slow diffusion of promising digital technologies, or the lack of enough research and development (R&D) activities [6, 11]. The spread of digital technologies and knowledge may also lead to structural change, which is "persistent change in the relative size of different sectors and occupations" [2, 14, 15]. This could lead to the decline of industries that use old technologies or are made useless by technological shifts [17]. According to Gorg and Greenaway [6], predicted positive digital spillovers are limited to local levels because of distance-related transaction costs, which are made worse in environments without adequate transportation and telecommunications infrastructure. Agglomeration economies can consequently limit network effects and information spillovers to a defined geographic area [4, 13, 14, 16], because elsewhere there are no infrastructures, administrations, or organizations designed to lower transaction costs and informational asymmetries. Three main spatial dynamics are embraced by these agglomeration economies, which operate within or across industries [8, 16].

Mobile Payment in Emerging Economies and the rest of the world.

Digitalization in Sub Saharan Africa: Regional Economic Outlook, April 2020

Localization economies or Marshall Externalities, which pertain to the digital spillovers between businesses that operate in the same sector or engage in comparable activities and are situated in the same location. Geographic closeness, for example, may encourage the diffusion of digital knowledge that enables more fluid commercial contacts in a particular sector.

Jacobs's externalities, which have to do with the digital spillovers between businesses that operate in various but connected industries in a specific place. For example, cross-industry links may benefit from network effects brought on by the implementation of a digital technology in a specific location, and *vice versa*.

Urbanization economies, which have to do with the digital spillovers brought on by urban size and density but are unrelated to the structure or complementarity of businesses, including externalities connected to connection infrastructure or the geographic concentration of the workforce with digital skills.

Localization (dis)economies may imbricate industrial and spatial spillovers. However, the possibility of local scale economies, Jacobs externalities, or urbanization economies raises the possibility that spatial aspects of digital spillovers may exist without being specific to any industry. This holds true for positive spillovers, such as those brought on by network effects or knowledge spillovers, as well as negative spillovers, which can spread across industries and have a spatial component. When businesses from the same location operating in new ICT-intensive industries spread digital technologies among one another, this causes structural change and the decline of "old industries" rendered obsolete by the digitization process. This is a striking example of negative spatial cross-industry spillovers [17, 18].

CONCLUSION

Where people and businesses are severely confined in their daily interactions by high transaction costs, informational asymmetries, a lack of infrastructure, and a high degree of unpredictability, digital technologies are called upon to play a crucial role. The Covid-19 issue has made these market flaws, which are prevalent throughout Africa, even worse. In the middle of a global health and economic crisis and with many obstacles to African development still in place, digitizing African economies opens up new ways to help the private sector grow and create jobs, especially for Small and Medium Enterprises (SMEs). African SMEs have not yet completely tapped into the possibilities of foundational digital technologies like email, internet, and mobile money. Although the adoption of mobile phone technology has aided in the proliferation of Internet-based innovations across the area, this trend is impeded by the widening digital divide and low levels of Internet access among businesses. The number of people who have access to the Internet in Africa in 2015 was less than 60%, with penetration rates as low as 5% in some nations like Niger, Sierra Leone, and Guinea-Bissau. According to surveys done by the World Bank between 2013 and 2018, less than 60% of SMEs used email for business, and less than 30% used websites. Beyond the immediate benefits of SMEs adopting digital technologies, empirical evidence suggests that their spread across industries and locations may not yet have reached the critical mass of users needed to bring about the expected positive network effects, knowledge spillovers, or economies of scale. But there is a chance that their growing spread will only help early adopters, which are usually large, highly productive businesses with enough capacity to absorb them, at the expense of ecosystems that are more fragile. This could lead to a loss of revenue, jobs, or the closing of a business.

REFERENCES

[1]   Patnam M, Yao W. The Real Effects of Mobile Money: Evidence from a Large-Scale Fintech Expansion. IMF working paper 2020.

[2]   Brezis E, Krugman P, Tsiddon D. Leap frogging in International Competition: A Theory of Cycles in National Technological Leadership. Am Econ Rev 1993; 83(5): 1211-9.

[3]   Rodrik D. An African growth miracle J Afr Econ 2016; 27(1): 10-27.

[4]   Cariolle J. International Connectivity and the Digital Divide in Sub-Saharan Africa 2020; P264.

[5]   Bertolini R. Telecommunication services in sub-Saharan Africa: An Analysis of Access and use in the Southern Volta Region in Ghana. Development Economics and Policy, Peter Lang Frankfurt 2002; p. 186.

[6]   Harrison B, Kelley MR, Gant J. Innovative firm behavior and local milieu: Exploring the intersection of agglomeration, firm effects, and technological change. Econ Geogr 1996; 72(3): 233-58. [http://dx.doi.org/10.2307/144400]

[7]   Paunov C, Rollo V. Has the internet fostered inclusive innovation in the developing world? World Dev 2016; 78: 587-609.

[http://dx.doi.org/10.1016/j.worlddev.2015.10.029]

[8]   Paunov C, Rollo V. Overcoming obstacles: The internet's contribution to firm development. World Bank Econ Rev 2015; 29 (Suppl. 1): S192-204.
[http://dx.doi.org/10.1093/wber/lhv010]

[9]   Sadowski BM, Maitland C, van Dongen J. Strategic use of the Internet by small- and medium-sized companies: An exploratory study. Inf Econ Policy 2002; 14(1): 75-93.
[http://dx.doi.org/10.1016/S0167-6245(01)00054-3]

[10]   Wakunuma K, Masika R. Cloud computing, capabilities and intercultural ethics: Implications for Africa. Telecomm Policy 2017; 41(7-8): 695-707.
[http://dx.doi.org/10.1016/j.telpol.2017.07.006]

[11]   Marsh IW, Rincon-Aznar A, Vecchi M, Venturini F. We see ICT spillovers everywhere but in the econometric evidence: A reassessment. Ind Corp Change 2017; 26(6): 1067-88.
[http://dx.doi.org/10.1093/icc/dtx008]

[12]   Aker JC, Mbiti IM. Mobile phones and economic development in africa. J Econ Perspect 2010; 24(3): 207-32.
[http://dx.doi.org/10.1257/jep.24.3.207]

[13]   Aker J, Blumenstock J. The economic impacts of new technologies in africa, in eds monga, c. & yifu lin. J The Oxford Handbook of Africa and Economics: Policies and Practices 2014; 2: 354-71.

[14]   Duncombe R, Heeks R. Enterprise across the digital divide: Information systems and rural microenterprise in Botswana. Journal of International Development. J Dev Stud 2002; 14(1): 61-74.

[15]   Harrison T, Waite K. A time-based assessment of the influences, uses and benefits of intermediary website adoption. Inf Manage 2006; 43(8): 1002-13.
[http://dx.doi.org/10.1016/j.im.2006.09.004]

[16]   Malmberg A, Malmberg B, Lundequist P. Agglomeration and firm performance: Economies of scale, localization, and urbanization among Swedish export firms. Environ Plann A 2000; 32(2): 305-21.
[http://dx.doi.org/10.1068/a31202]

[17]   Choi J, Dutz MA, Usman Z, Eds. The Future of Work in Africa: Harnessing the Potential of Digital Technologies for All. Washington, D.C.: Africa Development Forum Series, Agence Françoise de Development / The World Bank 2020.
[http://dx.doi.org/10.1596/978-1-4648-1445-7]

[18]   World bank africa's agricultural input landscape in sub-saharan africa 2019. Available from : https://www.worldbank.org/en/programs/africa-myths-and-facts/publication/afri-a-s-agriculturalinput-landscape-in-sub-saharan-africa

CHAPTER 5

Effect of Big Data on SMEs Performance

Mohammed Majeed[1,*]

[1] *Department of Marketing, Tamale Technical University, Tamale-Ghana*

Abstract: Due to the rapid increase in the amount and velocity of data transmission, the concept of "Big Data" has been on the minds of managers and decision-makers as a means to boost industrial productivity. As a result of the explosion in data volume and complexity brought on by new forms of advanced technology and a wide variety of market opportunities, a data-driven approach to business operations is now essential. This is becoming an increasingly important problem for small and medium-sized enterprises (SMEs), especially in Africa with inadequate infrastructure and resources. Notably, the majority of reports to date that explain how performance gain can be achieved have come from large, well-established firms, especially in developed countries, and there have been few attempts to study the main factors that affect SMEs' intention to adopt BD in developing countries like Africa. Therefore, the purpose of this research was to detect and explain the influence of BD on the performance of SMEs. Three categories of big data were identified in this chapter (structured, unstructured and semistructured). Big data's influence is that it helps SMEs better understand their clientele and respond to their needs through data-driven management and marketing strategies. On the other hand, BD is essential for SMEs to do market research and anticipate consumer actions. SMEs can benefit from BD since it improves their adaptability, efficiency, responsiveness, and the capacity to anticipate and meet client needs.

Keywords: Big Data, Structured, Semistructured, SMEs, Technology, Unstructured.

INTRODUCTION

The significant impact that SMEs have in both developed and developing nations is widely recognized. They have been lauded for their positive effects on economies and employment rates in developing nations. When it comes to creating jobs, fostering innovation, and advancing economic growth on a global scale, it's small and medium-sized businesses (SMEs) that are leading the way. Many organizations throughout the world are undergoing a digital transition, which is placing significant strain on both large and small companies to evaluate

[*] **Corresponding author Mohammed Majeed:** Department of Marketing, Tamale Technical University, Tamale-Ghana; E-mail: tunteya14june@gmail.com

their current methods of doing business and come up with novel approaches. The rate at which new data is being created has skyrocketed in recent years [1], and it shows no indications of slowing down. The Government Accountability Office [2] predicted that by 2025, between 25 and 50 billion devices would be linked to the Internet and generate data, and Bello-Orgaz *et al.* [3] projected that 2.5 exabytes of fresh data were being generated globally every day. Though they have access to a plethora of data, most businesses only make good use of only 5% of it [4]. A better understanding of how big data security analytics are being adopted could shed light on how best to employ this technology to efficiently detect security threats and thwart APTs. Additionally, small firms that implement this new technology may see an increase in data privacy, security, and accessibility [5].

When small and medium-sized enterprises (SMEs) generate and utilize big data, they can reap many benefits (Wand & Wang, 2020). Because of their proximity to their clientele, SMEs are well positioned to understand where their data comes from, what it's used for, and how much it's worth. But there are downsides for small and medium-sized enterprises (SMEs) when it comes to managing large data. Small and medium-sized businesses often struggle with insufficient funding [6]. Small and medium-sized businesses typically lack the necessary IT resources to properly collect and analyze data. Therefore, management is essential for SMEs to benefit from big data. SME may find "thinking big but starting small" to be a useful approach to big data. Some speculative research examines how BD affects the performance of large companies by enhancing the dynamic capability [7], supply chain management (Wamba *et al.*, 2020), or knowledge management [8]. These studies, however, have largely overlooked the widespread use of BD by SMEs. In fact, SMEs account for over 90% of businesses and 60%-70% of employment in OECD nations [5, 13], and BDAC has been recognized as a crucial tool for boosting SMEs' competitiveness [9].

Yet, there has been scant investigation into the factors that really matter to whether or not a company will decide to use this technology [10]. A company's bottom line can benefit from adopting big data practices, which are influenced by a number of external and internal factors [6]. However, by prioritizing the adoption determinants, stakeholders and policymakers can allocate resources more wisely during the adoption process [11]. The benefits of this new IT transformative tool have not gone unnoticed, and small and medium-sized enterprises (SMEs) across Africa have begun adopting BD in their operations [12]. However, limited study has been undertaken in this field as well as low adoption of BD by African firms [12]. Hence the goal of this chapter is to understand the effect of big data adoption on SMEs' performance.

CONTRIBUTIONS OF THE CHAPTER

This study may be of benefit to the practice of business since the findings may be of value to executives for establishing and implementing BD-based marketing strategies for improving sales revenues. As digital technology and metrics continue to evolve, firms aim to leverage BD technology and traditional marketing analytics to improve marketing efforts, decision-making, and financial outcomes. Applied knowledge may benefit from this research if it reveals actionable strategies that help marketing managers boost sales and accomplish other company goals.

LITERATURE

Big Data

"Big data is a novel technology that can digitally store a big amount of data," write Haleem *et al.* [3]. This method of computational analysis is useful for elucidating relationships, similarities, and differences. Marketing analytics, decisions, and strategies have all been affected by the advent of big data due to the amount, pace, and variety of this type of behavioral data [13]. The term "big data" (BD) was originally used to describe a broad analytical field that included all the many types of data that could be mined for insight and were distinguished by three characteristics: volume, velocity, and variety [14]. The phrase "big data" is used to refer to the vast volume of digital information (2.5 quintillion bytes of data created every day) generated from a wide range of sources, yet too unstructured to be examined by traditional relational database methods [10]. Big data is characterized by a combination of data volume, velocity, variety, and variety. By analyzing large amounts of data, businesses can learn more about their markets, consumers, and competitors [15]. Though the phrase "big data for small business" may sound contradictory, little firms are as in need of big data as their larger counterparts. Small and medium-sized enterprises (SMEs) can gain a competitive advantage by using big data to their advantage.

Types of Big Data

The types of big data as seen Fig. (1) include structured, unstructured and semi-structured.

Semistructured Data

This is the data type that has some type of structure or organization but does not reside in a standard database system like structured query language (Yan, Meng, Lu, & Li, 2017). Both types of information can exist in a semi-structured data set.

Although semi-structured data appears structured, its components are not defined in the same way as relational database tables are. For instance, an XML file contains semi-structured data [11]. Data that combines elements of both the unstructured and structured formats mentioned above is known as semi-structured data. In particular, it refers to information that does not fit neatly into any preexisting database but does have vital tags or information that separates apart individual parts of the material. This concludes our discussion of the various forms that big data might take. If SMEs need to transfer unstructured data between systems, especially if those systems have different underlying architectures, the firm can use a serialization language to do it. Information is typically written as plain text so that a wide variety of text editors can be used to analyze it and develop conclusions. Data serialization readers can be implemented on hardware with constrained processing resources and bandwidth because of the format's simplicity. It is between the two extremes, unstructured and structured data that semi-structured information exists. Metadata is essentially free-form data that describes other data. Information such as a device's ID, location, time stamp, email address, and email address can be passed down as semi-structured data. It may also take the form of a semantic tag appended to the information at a later time. Take the case of an electronic mail as an illustration. Connected to an email's content are the time it was sent, the sender's and recipient's email addresses, the IP address of the device the email was sent from, and other data. The content itself may not be organized, but these pieces make it possible for the information to be filed away in logical categories. Data that is only partially structured can be transformed into a valuable asset by joining the proper datasets. By tying together patterns with additional information, it can help in the development of machine learning and artificial intelligence.

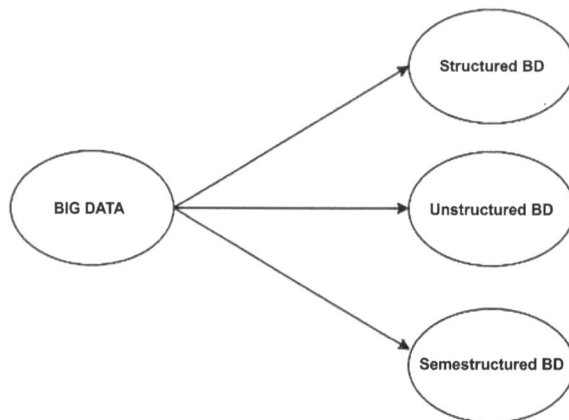

Fig. (1). Types of big data.

Structured Data

Information stored in a record's fields that is predetermined by the data model is called structured data. Conventional database management systems, such as those based on structured query language, are designed to store and retrieve structured data [9]. The word "structured data" refers to information that has a predetermined structure that allows for its organization, retrieval, and processing. Structured data refers to information characterized by a predefined format, facilitating its manipulation, retrieval, and storage. Skills in software engineering have advanced significantly over time, allowing for the development of methods for processing this type of data and deriving value from it. However, we now expect problems when the size of such data grows to a very large degree, with typical values being in the zettabyte range. Computer scientists have made considerable strides over time in creating methods for processing and extracting value from this type of data (when the format is known in advance). Problems arise, however, when the volume of such data rises to alarming proportions; current estimates put the normal volume at several zettabytes [11]. Simply said, structured data is information that is permanently stored in a designated area of a record. In this case, the schema ensures that all of the information shares the same characteristics. Another name for structured data is relational data. Data integrity is improved by using a single record to represent an entity, which is why the data is spread across several tables. A structured database is simple to populate, query, and examine. The information is uniformly presented. However, because every record must be changed to conform to the new format, enforcing a consistent structure makes it extremely difficult to make changes to the data. Numbers, dates, strings, *etc.* are all examples of structured data. The transactional information found on an online storefront can be categorized as a type of structured data.

The schemas that define the location and significance of each datum provide the road maps that structured data follows. One advantage of structured data is that it makes it easier to combine enterprise data and relational data. There is little prep work needed to have all sources be compatible because the relevant data dimensions have been defined and are in a common format.

Unstructured Data

Information that does not conform neatly to any preexisting data model, either because of its inherent variety or because it is dependent on a specific context (Seng & Ang, 2019). Unstructured data refers to information whose shape or organization is a mystery. Unstructured data is difficult to process because of its size and other characteristics that make it difficult to derive value from it.

Unstructured data typically comes from a heterogeneous data source that includes a wide variety of file types, such as text files, photos, videos, *etc* [11]. Modern businesses have access to a plethora of data, but the data is often in an unstructured format, making it difficult to extract useful insights. Size and diversity of it are much greater than those of structured data. Any set of information that lacks a defined structure is said to be unstructured. This information is difficult to process, interpret, and analyze because of its disorderly nature. It can evolve over time and is not rigidly defined. Here is where you will primarily encounter big data. Comments, tweets, shares, posts, videos watched on YouTube, and messages sent via WhatsApp are all examples of unstructured data.

Effect of Big Data on SMEs Performance

Small and medium-sized businesses (SMEs) can gain a lot from big data technologies, despite the common perception that only giant corporations use this type of technology (SMEs). With the help of this technology, businesses now have the means to handle massive amounts of both organized and unstructured data [12]. The integrity, confidentiality, and availability of data might all be enhanced if small businesses adopted big data security analytics [5]. As a revolutionary tool, big data allows businesses to gain important customer insights, establish trust, increase their bottom line, and gain a competitive edge [16]. According to reports, businesses can improve their performance with the help of big data analytics because it enables them to make informed strategic decisions [6, 17]. It is stated that big data analytics yields excellent outcomes across a variety of industries, and as such, big data analytics has become an integral part of the decision-making processes of agile organizations [18]. Big data analytics, for instance, is anticipated to reduce operating costs and improve quality of life in the healthcare sector, while the majority of retail organizations are actively expanding big data capabilities to improve customer-relationship management [16].

BD is critical to creating a more sustainable economy [12]. Cooperation and collaborations between IT, marketing, management, and core business operations were essential to the successful use of BD for profit by all organizations [12]. Throughout this chapter, the importance of using BD to drive marketing activities and strategies to enhance the customer experience was emphasized. It follows that businesses might utilize BD to enhance their competitiveness in the long run by enhancing their operational procedures and decision-making alternatives [12]. Gaining insights into client behavior that were previously unavailable using conventional data analysis techniques is a major advantage of Big Data. You may learn a lot about your customers' actions as they progress through your sales funnels with the help of data analytics solutions. While there is no absolute certainty in data analysis, it does equip SMEs with the resources necessary to tackle a wide variety of challenging situations. In addition to keeping tabs on customers, SMEs can also address concerns involving investors, partners, and suppliers. Real-time reporting provides a comprehensive picture of a company, allowing SMEs to make more informed decisions [19].

Using Big Data technologies, it is feasible to swiftly analyze massive amounts of data, allowing for the discovery of trends and patterns that would be impossible to uncover using conventional statistical methods and smaller data sets. Small and medium-sized enterprises (SMEs) can use this knowledge to fine-tune their offerings and better satisfy their clientele. Small and medium-sized businesses (SMBs) can also use Big Data to improve their marketing, consumer targeting, and the quality of the customer experience they offer [20]. It's clear that there are numerous ways in which big data might boost earnings. With the use of analytics, you may gain a thorough understanding of the client journey and discover novel ways to boost revenue. If you have access to reliable information, you may feel more comfortable introducing a new product or branching out your business, both of which could increase profits. Big data has been shown to enhance profits by an average of 8% for businesses who adopt it [19]. The data mined and evaluated from within the company and the industry can be used to discover untapped opportunities for growth and enhancement. In addition, because big data removes entry barriers, SMEs can more easily expand into new markets.

Many believe that big data analytics is a crucial skill for competitive success [6]. Improving a company's capacity for big data analytics should allow it to reach its full potential. This can be achieved by creating the capacity for big data analytics and determining the aspects that may aid in the development of this capacity. Organizational resources (big data analytics management), physical resources (IT infrastructure), and human resources (analytics skill or knowledge), all of which should be distinctive and unreplicable, come together to produce improved company performance in a big data-driven environment [14]. In numerous studies, authors explored the ways in which businesses are using BD to innovate and undergo a "data-driven" transformation. Organizations are realizing the value of big data and its ability to transform their huge amounts of data into actionable insight, improved operational efficiency, and sustainable competitive advantage [12]. A crucial change in technology that has had an enormous effect on advertising is the rise of Big Data (BD) [5]. The necessity to maximize the benefits of BD and its usage in business-to-business (B2B) settings has received a great deal of attention from marketers and scholars in the field of industrial marketing [10]. Business intelligence (BD) is a marketing term for discussing companies' reactions to data gathering, storage, and utilization. Big data also simplifies team management for SMBs. Experts in the field can help you determine who among your staff members is the most valuable, and who among them could benefit from more time, money, or education. The reason for this is because the insights generated by analytics systems may be used to boost productivity and maintain a positive work environment.

Businesses that make use of big data are more likely to be efficient round-the-clock because they are better able to anticipate and meet the needs of their consumers and because they have a deeper understanding of their customers' profiles, needs, and wishes. Everything gets done on time, which ensures satisfied customers and more money in the bank.

The prospects presented by big data for SMEs to grow and become more competitive in the modern business environment are vast. Despite initial concerns, small and medium-sized enterprises (SMEs) can learn and benefit greatly from Big Data technologies. Small and medium-sized enterprises (SMEs) can increase profits and maintain a competitive edge by leveraging Big Data with the correct infrastructure and resources [20].

With the use of big data, businesses may provide superior service to their clients. Finding out what people believe and do in the marketplace is made possible by having access to data as it happens. When you have this data, you may use it to improve your company. Big data analytics-based personalized customer service will help you connect with customers on a more meaningful level and deliver tailored service that boosts revenue. Businesses are just beginning to realize the potential of big data in helping marketers find and connect with customers and prospects. Disgruntled clients may soon stop patronizing small and medium-sized enterprises (SMEs) that refuse to adopt analytics. Small businesses are increasingly turning to big data as a customer service tool [19].

IMPLICATIONS

Big data is quite beneficial for small and big companies alike. Consider investing in big data to enjoy these benefits. Using Big Data analytics, companies could increase their revenue by generating more sales leads. Many businesses are turning to it to learn how well their products and services are performing on the market and how their customers are responding. In this way, they can make informed decisions about where to invest their time and resources. Most people used to think that big data was only for big business. But, as time goes on, it is clear that this technology is for even SMEs. Big data can have a significant impact on cost-cutting in SMEs by identifying expensive processes and redundant workflows. With the latest data, SMEs can find areas of the business to scale up or down. This can have long-term financial benefits. With the help of Big Data analytics tools, businesses around the world are improving their digital marketing strategies by utilising and processing data from social media platforms. Insights from Big Data allow companies to improve their products and services based on customer pain points. Big Data combines data from multiple sources to produce actionable insights. Companies can save time and money by using analytics tools to filter out redundant data.

CONCLUSION

Data gathering and analysis have become vital organizational strategies in light of the exponential growth in data volume and complexity brought on by new, cutting-edge technology and the variety of today's marketplaces. This is becoming an increasingly pressing concern for SMEs, particularly in Africa with inadequate infrastructure and resources. Hence the goal of this chapter is to understand the effect of big data adoption SMEs' performance. Structured data, unstructured data, and semi-structured data are the three main categories used to describe large data. Big data prepares for virtually every knowledge a business could be looking for, whether the analytics being used are predictive, diagnostic, descriptive, or prescriptive. Data analysis and harvesting down are skills that have been around for decades, if not centuries, making them a crucial foundation for the field of big data analytics. Structured, semi-structured, and unstructured data all exist within the realm of applications. In contrast, structured data is well-defined and follows a rigid framework. While semi-structured data defies classification, it nonetheless exhibits useful characteristics for businesses. Languages for serializing data are used to transform data items into a string of bytes. To name a few: XML, JSON, and YAML. Data that is unstructured can be interpreted in many different ways. An application contains all three types of information. It's impossible to create innovative and engaging apps without all three of them.

Businesses can collect data from numerous sources in real time using in-memory analytics. With the use of big data tools, analysts can quickly assess data and take prompt action based on their findings. The efficiency of operations may be improved with the use of big data techniques. Using these technologies, workers will have more time to focus on more complex jobs that require their critical thinking. Companies might benefit from a deeper understanding of the market thanks to big data analysis. By analyzing consumer spending habits, for instance, manufacturers can zero in on product demand and design around it. Because of this, you'll be able to exceed the competition. Companies driven by big data can better serve supplier networks and business-to-business (B2B) communities. Successful outcomes need the use of complex contextual knowledge, and this is made feasible by big data. With the use of big data, businesses can better target their advertising dollars toward consumers who are most likely to actually buy their products. Companies can better match customer expectations and encourage brand loyalty with the help of these techniques, which are informed by data collected through various marketing channels.

RECOMMENDATION FOR ACTION

The suggested next steps will aid businesses in gaining the information necessary to create successful BD-based marketing strategies that boost sales revenues. As part of a comprehensive BD-based marketing strategy to boost sales revenues, it is recommended that marketing leaders hire marketing strategists, improve the analytical skills of current managers, set aside funds in the marketing budget for predictive analytics, and incorporate omnichannel customer engagements by marketing alignment with sales.

Case of MYBank in China

China, the largest fintech market in the world, has been at the forefront of fintech growth, and virtual banking is only one of its many innovative aspects. The main four tech companies in China—Alibaba, Baidu, Tencent, and JD—have entered the financial services market thanks to digital technology and big data. 11 new licenses for privately owned banks were granted by China's banking authority between 2014 and 2016, one of which went to MYbank. Three banks (MYbank, WeBank, and XW Bank) have established a wider reach among millions of small and medium-sized firms (SMEs) by trying to attract private money into the Chinese financial services sector.

MYbank, which has its headquarters in Hangzhou, Zhejiang province (in southeast China), was established in 2015 by Ant Group, a subsidiary of Alibaba, with a 30% ownership stake in a joint venture made up of a number of private companies. To provide credit to SMEs and control risks, MYbank leverages big data, machine learning, and the related flexible risk management strategy. About 80% of MYbank's 20 million SME customers have never borrowed money from a bank before, and the company keeps its nonperforming loan (NPL) ratio at about 1%.

For SMEs and people in urban and rural locations, MYbank offers funding. Its operational costs are significantly cheaper than those of the conventional brick-and-mortar banking model thanks to its data-and cloud-based architecture and lack of physical branches. By utilizing its big data analytics-driven credit-profiling tools (such as e-commerce and cash flow), MYbank is able to approve modest loans for individuals and businesses round-the-clock, every day of the week, giving the Chinese people access to money and liquidity.

The combined SMEs handled by MYbank in 2019 totaled 20.9 million, the capital adequacy ratio was 16.4%, and the NPL ratio was 1.3 percent. MYbank's total assets in 2019 were RMB 139.6 billion ($20 billion), the average loan size was RMB 31,000 ($4,500), and the average loan size was RMB 31,000.

REFERENCES

[1]   Bello-Orgaz G, Jung JJ, Camacho D. Social big data: Recent achievements and new challenges. Inf Fusion 2016; 28: 45-59.
[http://dx.doi.org/10.1016/j.inffus.2015.08.005] [PMID: 32288689]

[2]   Government Accountability Office Internet of things, Status and implications of an increasingly connected world.gao 2017. Available from : https://www.gao.gov/products/GAO-17-75

[3]   Haleem A, Javaid M, Khan IH, Vaishya R. Significant applications of big data in COVID-19 pandemic. Indian J Orthop 2020; 54(4): 526-8.
[http://dx.doi.org/10.1007/s43465-020-00129-z] [PMID: 32382166]

[4]   Zakir J, Seymour T, Berg K. Big data analytics. Issues Inf Syst 2015; 16(2): 81. Available from : http://www.iacis.org/

[5]   Rassam MA, Maarof MA, Zainal A. Big data analytics adoption for cybersecurity: A review of current solutions, requirements, challenges and trends. J inf assur secur 2017; 12(4): 124-45. Available from : http://www.mirlabs.org/jias/index.html

[6]   Ghasemaghaei M, Hassanein K, Turel O. Increasing firm agility through the use of data analytics: The role of fit. Decis Support Syst 2017; 101: 95-105.
[http://dx.doi.org/10.1016/j.dss.2017.06.004]

[7]   Mikalef P, Krogstie J, Pappas IO, Pavlou P. Exploring the relationship between big data analytics capability and competitive performance: The mediating roles of dynamic and operational capabilities. Inf Manage 2020; 57(2): 103169.
[http://dx.doi.org/10.1016/j.im.2019.05.004]

[8]   Ferraris A, Mazzoleni A, Devalle A, Couturier J. Big data analytics capabilities and knowledge management: Impact on firm performance. Manage Decis 2019; 57(8): 1923-36.
[http://dx.doi.org/10.1108/MD-07-2018-0825]

[9]   Latifi M-A, Nikou S, Bouwman H. Business model innovation and firm performance: Exploring causal mechanisms in SMEs. Technovation 2021; 107: 102274.
[http://dx.doi.org/10.1016/j.technovation.2021.102274]

[10]   Kharat AT, Singhal S. A peek into the future of radiology using big data applications. Indian J Radiol Imaging 2017; 27(2): 241-8.
[http://dx.doi.org/10.4103/ijri.IJRI49316] [PMID: 28744087]

[11]   Taylor D. What is Big Data?introduction, types, characteristics,examples. guru99 2022. Available from : https://www.guru99.com/what-is-big-data.html

[12]   Majeed M, Alhassan S, Arko-Cole N. Role, characteristics and critical success factors of big data (bd): Implications for Marketing in Africa. In: Adeola O, Edeh JN, Hinson RE, Eds. Digital Business in Africa. Cham: Palgrave Studies of Marketing in Emerging Economies. Palgrave Macmillan 2022.
[http://dx.doi.org/10.1007/978-3-030-93499-6_10]

[13]   Erevelles S, Fukawa N, Swayne L. Big data consumer analytics and the transformation of marketing. J Bus Res 2016; 69(2): 897-904.
[http://dx.doi.org/10.1016/j.jbusres.2015.07.001]

[14]   Chen DQ, Preston DS, Swink M. How the Use of Big Data Analytics Affects Value Creation in Supply Chain Management. J Manage Inf Syst 2015; 32(4): 4-39.
[http://dx.doi.org/10.1080/07421222.2015.1138364]

[15]   Kitchin R, McArdle G. What makes Big Data, Big Data? Exploring the ontological characteristics of 26 datasets. Big Data Soc 2016; 3(1).
[http://dx.doi.org/10.1177/2053951716631130]

[16]   Tweney D. Walmart Scoops up Inkiru to Bolster Its 'Big Data' Capabilities Online Available from : https://venturebeat.com/2013/06/10/walmart-scoops-up-inkiru-to-bolster-its-big-data-capabilities-online/

[17]   Brands K. Big Data and Business Intelligence for Management Accountants. Strateg Financ 2014; 96: 64-5.

[18]   Hagel J. Bringing analytics to life. J Account 2015; 219: 24.

[19]   Fuggle L. Big data for small businesses: How to leverage big data for big results. 2022. Available from : https://blog.hubspot.com/marketing/big-data-for-small-businesses

[20]   Celebi A. SMEs can benefit from Big Data just like an enterprise dataconomy. 2022. Available from : https://dataconomy.com/2022/03/big-data-benefits-for-SMEs/

CHAPTER 6

Digitization Initiative and Digital Transformation for African Telecom Service Providers

Sophia Jonathan Machemba[1,*] and **Parag Shukla**[2]

¹ The Maharaja Sayajirao University of Baroda, Pratapgunj, Vadodara, Gujarat-390002, India

² Department of Commerce, and Business Management, Faculty of Commerce The Maharaja Sayajirao University of Baroda, Pratapgunj, Vadodara, Gujarat-390002, India

Abstract: Technology breakthroughs brought unforeseen competition among telecom operators in Africa. Digitization and digital transformation were the results of the revolution in technology. The study uses a literature review to discuss the digital initiative and digital transformation of African telecom operators' changes and challenges. Although Africa is still stepping ahead to effectively engage itself in digitization and technology, especially in the telecommunications industry, the outcome of digitization is to bring out the company's profit, gain more customers through experience, and increase efficiency and effectiveness. The results show that customization, sales optimization networks, single-run access networks, and power machine learning are positive trends that African telecom operators must focus on to bring about changes in the telecommunications industry. The managerial implication of the study is that telecom operators must invest in technology and infrastructure that facilitate digitization and digital transformation to operate accordingly.

Keywords: African telecom operators, Digitization, Digital transformation.

INTRODUCTION

The telecommunications industry is now one of the main sectors responsible for life support. This fact gives impetus to the formation of completely new needs, that did not exist before telemetry services based on machine-to-machine technology, virtual data warehousing, *etc* [1]. Hence, digitization is not just a threat, it also offers telecom companies an opportunity to rebuild their market positions, reimagine their business systems, and create innovative offerings for customers [2]. This has made resources more accessible online for distance research, providing better access, ease of use for the community and beyond, and easier access to information through digitization and facilitating fragile resources that are difficult to access [3-6]. All these are the needs of the digitization of the

---

* **Corresponding author Sophia Jonathan Machemba:** The Maharaja Sayajirao University of Baroda, Pratapgunj, Vadodara, Gujarat-390002, India; E-mail: sjmachemba@gmail.com

Mohammed Majeed, Abdul-Razak Abubakari, Awini Gideon and Jayadatta S. (Eds.)

telecom sector. Telecommunication service providers invest in transforming the telecommunication service lifecycle journey into digital, digitizing, searching for a service or product, purchase, using a service or product, after-sales support, and feedback [7].

However, customer expectations create an additional load on the telecommunication sector to change their system to open more digital platforms and windows for telecommunication service providers to invest in the core infrastructure to meet customer expectations from a performance perspective [4]. Therefore, digitization prompts digital transformation, while digital transformation in the telecommunications industry is based on creating innovation and being customer-centric [8].

Additionally, infrastructure access to telecommunication and services is essential for the digitalization of the economy [9]. Transforming capability and digital transformation are based on artificial intelligence, big data analytics, and business intelligence [10, 11]. The big challenge telecommunication companies have is: i) how to take advantage of the opportunity in digital disruption through innovation management and ii) how to accelerate internal digital transformation led by the digital leadership capability [12].

So, this study will prompt discussion regarding the digitization initiative and its positive contribution to the sector. At the same time, the study looks ahead to understand digital transformation and its processes in the telecom sector. Also, telecom operators must adjust to the technological revolution (digitization and digital transformation). Furthermore, they may employ digital development to deliver high-quality service, meet consumer expectations, and foster a great customer experience.

LITERATURE REVIEW

The Context of the African Telecom Industry

In the context of Africa, in the last five years, there has been the fastest telecom growth worldwide, which has transformed fundamental aspects of social and business life. Mobile subscriber growth remains the fastest in the African region, and the penetration of services is reaching a larger number of customers. Similarly, based on the GSMA (2020) report, by the year 2019, more than 477 million people, equivalent to 45 percent of the entire population had subscribed to mobile services, and this number is projected to reach 50 percent by the year 2025. Thus, to capitalize on the positive telecom market growth, telecommunication companies are tasked with creating marketing strategies that appeal to many potential consumers and solve a variety of challenges.

Major Telecom Operators in Africa

Orange Egypt is the largest telecommunication company on the continent. It generates $11 billion annual revenue. The company has taken the lead in constructing telecommunications infrastructure, having installed underground coverage stations throughout Cairo and other major Egyptian population centers.

Based in South Africa, the MTN Group offers telecommunication services not only in Africa but also in many European and Asian countries. The firm has been particularly successful in Nigeria, where it provides 35% of all telecommunication services. Combined with earnings in 19 other countries, this has allowed the MTN Group to generate $10.92 billion in revenue, the second-highest figure for any telecom firm on the continent.

With more than 55 million customers, Vodacom has one of the largest subscriber networks on the continent. It provides telecommunication services in 40 different countries, including Mozambique, Nigeria, Zambia, Angola, the Democratic Republic of the Congo, and Cameroon. It is particularly successful in the country where it is headquartered, South Africa - where it has 23 million subscribers and a market share of 58%. With such a large and widespread network of operations, Vodacom earns $5.4 billion in revenue each year. The company's success is due largely to its valuable promotions and flexible, affordable pricing structure.

A subsidiary of the Bharti Airtel company, Airtel Africa has 78 million subscribers on the African continent. It has been particularly successful in Nigeria and Ghana, which together account for 60 million of its customers. It has become popular among business professionals and others who have to travel from country to country. This is a consequence of no small part of its One Network plan, which allows subscribers to buy a service plan in one country and use it at the same price in other countries.

Concept of Digital Transformation

Digital transformation is a combination of both procedures of digitization and digital innovation with the intention of improving existing products with advanced abilities [13]. Adaptation and innovation processes are shaped by the interplay between collective identity and the nature of digital work and innovation [14]. Innovative approach to business transformation is driven by the digital economy [15] along with new entrants and new business models which threaten the survival of both incumbents and deeply established ideals and practices, that lead to new business models, new users, and innovative experiments [14]. In order to plan and execute digital transformation, organisations must have a clear strategy and place "digital" at the heart of their business strategies [16]. The digital transformation process is required to integrate general management and information systems research in an effort to comprehensively understand firms that attempt to adopt digital technologies [17], by triggering significant changes to its properties through combinations of information, computing, communication, and connectivity technologies [18]. Hence, there is a need to complement existing scholarship in domains such as information and communication technologies for development (ICT4D); mobile for development (M4D), or data for development (D4D) [19].

In its traditional sense, digital transformation refers to the use of computer and internet technology for a more efficient and effective economic value creation process [20], while in a broader sense, it refers to changes that the new technology has on the whole, on how we operate, interact, and configure, and how wealth is created within this system [20]. It offers workers greater freedoms, such as working hours and working models that suit them. Work times and locations, as well as task fulfilment, are becoming increasingly flexible and placing greater demands on employee skills and qualifications [21]. Designing new ways of doing things that generate new sources of value is also one advantage of digitisation [16]. Digital transformation is not simply applying digital technologies to change something in a business. At best, this can be considered a digital change, which may be beneficial to the business but not transformational. For instance, companies can apply digital technologies to accelerate business processes, eliminate inefficiencies, reduce costs, or even sell more, but these projects are not truly transformational [22]. The transformational effect of new digital technologies can be seen in all businesses [23]. New roles, professions, markets, and services have developed due to this digital transformation [24].

Wing Eyes African Telecom Service Operators Must Look for

As technology becomes a keyholder of transformation, which is required in terms of transition, there will be changes in the way the communication industry grows in the coming decade.

The Internet of Things is driving digital transformation in the telecom sector in two ways. First, as internet-connected devices become more popular, the need for fast and reliable connections increases. Secondly, utilizing the IoT creates ease for telecom providers to monitor the various communications bases remotely [25-27]. IoT enables service providers to provide greater means of communication between devices and people. IoT attempts to achieve the highest level of efficiency, seamless business processes, and increased revenue. Also, it can be used in various sectors, including energy, technology, and healthcare.

Visualization provides the ability to comprehend huge amounts of data, allows the perception of emergent properties that were not anticipated, enables problems with the data itself to become immediately apparent, and facilitates the understanding of both large-scale and small-scale features of the data. Additionally, it makes it easier to comprehend the data's large- and small-scale properties [28]. Hence, effective visualizations will allow a scientist to both understand their own data and communicate their insights to others [29]. Visual exploration of massive data sets arising from telecommunication networks and services is one of the challenges [30].

Big data operators [31] as stated, are facing disruptive technologies, rapidly changing business rules, and an intensified regulatory environment, leading to eroding service margins. In this scenario, the only stabilizing factor for telecom operators is revenue generated from data provisioning and driving value from this data. Telecom operators can use advanced analytics on customer and network data to generate a real-time view of customer preferences and network efficiency. This could empower them to make near-real-time and fact-based decisions and hence enable a forward-looking, focused, decisive, and action-oriented culture in the company. Hence, telecommunications data is generated in the many different operational systems used and could be generally classified into three main types: (1) customer contractual data; (2) call detail data; and (3) network data [32].

An electronic payment (e-payment), in short, can basically be defined as paying for goods or services on the internet or through a gateway to pay an amount. It includes all financial operations using electronic devices, such as computers, smartphones, or tablets. E-payments can be made in many ways, like credit or debit card payments or bank transfers [33 - 35]. Mobile advertising refers to any form of advertising that appears on smartphones and mobile devices such as tablets and e-readers. It includes all the interactive channels that are used by advertisers to communicate or promote brand information, news, or offers through mobile devices or networks [36].

Challenges of African Telecom Operators Toward Digital Transformation

Telecommunication infrastructures promote economic growth and development in Africa by a composite index of telecommunication computed from mobile lines, fixed lines, and internet access penetration [37]. Hence, there is a need to promote inclusive and holistic policies that will enhance digital provision, economic growth, and development simultaneously in Africa. Also, an increase in telecommunication infrastructure will encourage aggregate output and standard of living to move in the same direction in Africa [38], as will consumer protection issues [39].

Over the past years, when African operators think about the impact of clouds, Cloud computing has grown to become a truly dispensable aspect of the modern IT infrastructure [40]. Initially, organizations rely on cloud services for data storage among the backup needs and organizations increasingly rely on cloud computing to deliver nearly core services [41]. While increasing the adaptation of 5G, Artificial Intelligence, and the Internet of Things (IoT), cloud computing has further propelled.

Digital inclusion is fragmented and uncoordinated due to duplication of resources, time-wasting, and high costs [42]. Mobile operators therefore need to adapt to people's behavior on mobile across their customers' lifecycles rather than forcing their customers to correspond to their traditional portfolio of services and channels, such as calls or in-store visits. Increasing personalization may entail decoupling those people and technologies that touch the customer from the back-office and network technology. This alone represents a transformational challenge [43, 44].

DISCUSSION

Digital Initiative toward the African Telecom Sector

Consider the example of Airtel Tanzania, which has adopted digitization across its operation to serve an overgrown number of mobile users, automating and digitizing based on distribution and providing customers with all the information needed by 'My Airtel Mobile App', this app is used to understand the customer better, and the company is cheering up to engage with the consumer more effectively.

Digitization is not only about automation; the company must look at the other side, like customer-focused digitization, which is the creation of a new model for consumers and the company to interact with the consumer in very different ways.

Customization is aided by digitization, customization and digitization of social and analytical tools help telecom operators improve efficiency and save time and also to understand user preference for both product and service offerings rather than a one-size-fits-all approach, hence, it helps reduce the amount of customer data needed to remain safe and secure.

Implementation of the sales optimization network will help telecom operators improve the performance of their networks, reduce operation and capital expenditures, and provide a better customer experience. Digitization enables telecom operators to make large changes to the network in large numbers (Figs. **1** & **2**).

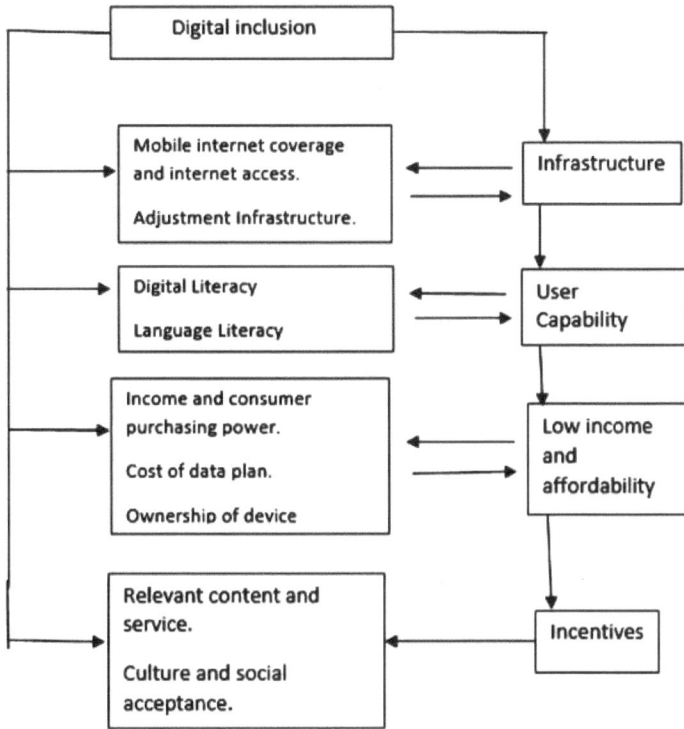

Fig. (1). Digital inclusion variables telecommunication must adopt, access and application: digital inclusion (gsma intelligence, [45]).

Fig. (2). Model of digitization initiative in the telecom sector (modified from siddiqui *et al.* [26], and srinidhi *et al.* [27]).

Implementation of the Singe Ran, or Single Radio Access Network, means one piece of equipment under a particular spectrum can have multiple technologies, while telecom operators must use analytical distribution management to put truck distribution incentives in high-sim card-demanding areas (Using data analytics to customize service for subscribers).

Due to the changing nature of consumer behavior, telecom operators must operate and understand at the consumer level, not at the mass segment level. To succeed, this telecom company needs a lot of power from machine learning.

CHANGES THAT DIGITIZATION BRINGS TO THE AFRICAN TELECOMMUNICATION SECTOR

Virtualized communications and a cloud-based deployment make it easier for telcos to manage traffic without burning too much of a hole in their pockets. The source of contents and the data center sometimes affect the demand pattern from the optical layer. Hence, there is a disparity between demand and supply; some data centers carry an "Elephant, "or a huge amount of data, while the demand for consumer links will be much smaller. So 5G will completely revolutionize the customer experience through strong connectivity and the expansion of the ability and functionality of the Internet of Things (IOT) [46 - 48]. We believe that 5G will not only enable new experiences for consumers but also create new opportunities for businesses of all sizes and types, helping them drive innovation and efficiency [49, 50].

Diversification of digital services. Mobile service operators must adjust and know how to expand their service packages to offer new suites of digital services, address new vertical markets with strong earnings growth potential, and focus on opportunities, for example, around smart cities, healthcare, industrial manufacturing, and more [51 - 53]. They must also match the kind of service compartment that best matches their competencies and, basically, modify their functionality to manage these branching service ranges while reducing operable convolution efficiently.

To redefine customer engagement and win the race for customer loyalty and mindshare, telecom industry players will need to increasingly deploy features and tools that deliver delightful digital experiences. This is especially important as customers now expect the high-quality digital experiences, they receive in one industry to be matched by companies in other sectors [54].

Transformation of customer expectations into digital means through:

1. Customer interaction due to their wants and needs.

2. Easier mode of payment.

3. Awareness among consumers to understand the features of the product and service.

Robotic Process Automation is being used for repetitive tasks and processes, enabling ease and agility for report generation, price tracking, back-office tasks, and responding to customers. With RPA solutions, employees can focus on essential functions that require their attention while leaving rote tasks to automated technologies.

The network's ability to respond to network changes in real-time while keeping pace with a business's evolving technology needs is called an **"agile network"**. Digital transformation brings positive changes to the telecom sector by allowing the adaptation of networking and the influx of new devices while remaining secure, flexible, and manageable.

CONCLUSION

Digitization and digital transformation have many impacts on the telecommunications industry in Africa. Internet of Things, Visualization, Big data, and E-payment, are the factors African telecom operators must look ahead to compete in the world market and adjust to the new version and revolution of technology. Hence, massive initiatives for Africa's telecom operators in this sector must come up with different ways to sustain the telecom sector toward digitization, such as automating digitizing, customization, sales optimization networks, single-run access networks, and the advancement of machine learning. Additionally, digitization and digital transformation are where African telecom operators must compete with other telecom operators worldwide. However, virtualized communications and cloud-based deployment, diversification of digital services, redefining customer engagement, and agile networks are the changes digitization and digital transformation bring to the telecom industry, both for operators and customers.

REFERENCES

[1]   Ahmad H, Mustafa H. The impact of artificial intelligence, big data analytics and business intelligence on transforming capability and digital transformation in Jordanian telecommunication firms. Int J Data Netw Sci 2022; 6(3): 727-32.
[http://dx.doi.org/10.5267/j.ijdns.2022.3.009]

[2]   Ahmed A, Aziz A, Muneeb M. Electronic payment system: A complete guide. J Multidiscip Res 2019; 1(2): 1-17.
[http://dx.doi.org/10.33888//jms.2019.121]

[3]   Attaran M. The impact of 5G on the evolution of intelligent automation and industry digitization. J Ambient Intell Humaniz Comput 2021; 0123456789.
[http://dx.doi.org/10.1007/s12652-020-02521-x] [PMID: 33643481]

[4]   Awadhia J, Al , Obeidata B. The impact of customer service digitalization on customer satisfaction: Evidence from telecommunication industry. Int J Data Netw Sci 2021; 5(4): 831-6.
[http://dx.doi.org/10.5267/j.ijdns.2021.x.002]

[5]   Bernat L, Bourassa F, Brocca J, *et al.* Key issues for digital transformation in the g20 from the oecd

centre for entrepreneurship, SMEs, local development and tourism, and deborah roseveare from the oecd directorate for education and skills, provided valuable comments. January, 2017.

[6]   Bumann J, Peter M. Action fields of digital transformation–a review and comparative analysis of digital transformation maturity models and frameworks. Digitalisierung Und Andere Innovationsformen Im Management 2019; 2: 13-40.

[7]   Caylar P, Ménard A. How telecom companies can win in the digital revolution. 2016. Available from: http://www.mckinsey.com/business-functions/digital-mckinsey/our-insights/how-telecom-companies-c an-win-in-the-digital-revolution

[8]   CII. Cloud and the age of continuous disruption. The journey of digital transformation 2021.

[9]   Data G. Why 5G is important for enterprises. Infosys 2019; (April): 24.

[10]   David OO. Nexus between telecommunication infrastructures, economic growth and development in Africa: Panel vector autoregression (P-VAR) analysis. Telecomm Policy 2019; 43(8): 101816. [http://dx.doi.org/10.1016/j.telpol.2019.03.005]

[11]   David OO, Grobler W. Information and communication technology penetration level as an impetus for economic growth and development in Africa. Ekon Istraz 2020; 33(1): 1394-418. [http://dx.doi.org/10.1080/1331677X.2020.1745661]

[12]   The Internet of Things. Available from: Available from: https://www2.deloitte.com/us/en/pages/ consulting/topics/the-internet-of-things.html.

[13]   Opportunities in Telecom Sector : Arising from Big Data. *Aegis, School of Business, School of Data Science*. School of Telecommunicationn 2015; 32.

[14]   Deloitte. 2016. Available from: https://www2.deloitte.com/

[15]   Dwivedi Y K, Ismagilova E, Hughes D L, *et al.* Setting the future of digital and social media marketing research: Perspectives and research propositions. IJIM 2021; 59: 102168. [http://dx.doi.org/10.1016/j.ijinfomgt.2020.102168]

[16]   Fatonah S, Yulandari A, Wibowo FW. A review of e-payment system in e-commerce. J Phys Conf Ser 2018; 1140(1): 012033. [http://dx.doi.org/10.1088/1742-6596/1140/1/012033]

[17]   Feyen E, Frost J, Gambacorta L, Natarajan H, Saal M. Fintech and the digital transformation of financial services: implications for market structure and public policy. BIS Papers No 117 2021.

[18]   Frennert S. Hitting a moving target: Digital transformation and welfare technology in Swedish municipal eldercare. Disabil Rehabil Assist Technol 2021; 16(1): 103-11. [http://dx.doi.org/10.1080/17483107.2019.1642393] [PMID: 31348681]

[19]   Furinto A. The effect of digital leadership and innovation management for incumbent telecommunication company in the digital disruptive era. Int J Eng Adv Technol 2018; 7(29). [http://dx.doi.org/10.14419/ijet.v7i2.29.13142]

[20]   Gopalalah S. 5G: The Catalyst to Digital Revolution in India. Deloitte 2018.

[21]   GSMA: Digital inclusion Report Available from: http://www.ncbi.nlm.nih.gov/pubmed/19547787

[22]   Kabakchieva D. usiness Intelligence Applications and Data Mining Methods in Telecommunications : A Literature Review. 2009. Available from: http://research.uni-sofia.bg/jspui/handle/10506/241

[23]   Kesharwani S. Unit-5 E-Payment. New Delhi: Indira Gandhi National Open University 2021; pp. 85-110.

[24]   Koutsofios EE, North SC, Truscott R, Keim DA. Visualizing large-scale telecommunication networks and services. Proceedings of the IEEE Visualization Conference, November. 24-29 October 1999; San Francisco, CA, USA. 1999; pp. 457-61. [http://dx.doi.org/10.1109/VISUAL.1999.809930]

[25]   Kumar KSA. A new approach of CLOUD…. Srivastava & Kumar 2011; 7(2): 145-53.

[26]   Limited, I. (n.d.). Perspective Telecom Companies and.

[27]   Mandviwalla M, Flanagan R. Small business digital transformation in the context of the pandemic. Eur J Inf Syst 2021; 30(4): 359-75.
[http://dx.doi.org/10.1080/0960085X.2021.1891004]

[28]   McKinsey & Company. The recovery will be digital. 2020. Available from: https://www.mckinsey. com/~/media/McKinsey/Business Functions/McKinsey Digital/Our Insights/How six companies are using technology and data to transform themselves/The-next-normal-the-recovery-will-be-digital.pdf

[29]   Mwakatumbula HJ, Moshi GC, Mitomo H. Consumer protection in the telecommunication sector: A comparative institutional analysis of five African countries. Telecomm Policy 2019; 43(7): 101808.
[http://dx.doi.org/10.1016/j.telpol.2019.02.002]

[30]   Ndemo B, Weiss T. Making sense of africa's emerging digital transformation and its many futures. Afr J Manag 2017; 3(3-4): 328-47.
[http://dx.doi.org/10.1080/23322373.2017.1400260]

[31]   Patterson G, Bharti S, Weinelt B. Digital Transformation of Industries. 2017. Available from: http://reports.weforum.org/digital-transformation/wp-content/blogs.dir/94/mp/files/pages/files/dti-telec ommunications-industry-white-paper.pdf

[32]   Personal M, Archive R. Rules, institutions, or both? Estimating the drivers of telecommunication investment in Latin America. MPRA Paper 105165, University Library of Munich, Germany 2021.

[33]   Proskura NV. Digital Transformation of Economy. Need for Integrated Introduction of Availability Rate of Telecommunication Services Within the Sustainable Development of Rural Territories 2020; 147(151): 302-7.

[34]   Ragnedda M, Mutsvairo B. Accepted Manuscript This chapter has been accepted for publication and undergone full peer review but has not been through the copyediting, typesetting, pagination and proofreading process which may lead to differences between this version and the Versi 2018.

[35]   Reddy SK, Reinartz W. Digital transformation and value creation: Sea change ahead. NIM MIR 2017; 9(1): 10-7.
[http://dx.doi.org/10.1515/gfkmir-2017-0002]

[36]   Santiago. (2021). technologies new future Thank you for your interest in. 2021.

[37]   Siddiqui S, Shakir MZ, Khan AA, Dey I. Internet of Things (IoT) enabled architecture for social distancing during pandemic. FRCMN 2021; 2: 614166.
[http://dx.doi.org/10.3389/frcmn.2021.614166]

[38]   Sicari S, Rizzardi A, Coen-Porisini A. 5G In the internet of things era: An overview on security and privacy challenges. Comput Netw 2020; 179: 107345.
[http://dx.doi.org/10.1016/j.comnet.2020.107345]

[39]   Soluk J, Kammerlander N. Digital transformation in family-owned Mittelstand firms: A dynamic capabilities perspective. Eur J Inf Syst 2021; 30(6): 676-711.
[http://dx.doi.org/10.1080/0960085X.2020.1857666]

[40]   Soto-Acosta P. COVID-19 pandemic: Shifting digital transformation to a high-speed gear. Inf Syst Manage 2020; 37(4): 260-6.
[http://dx.doi.org/10.1080/10580530.2020.1814461]

[41]   Sraml Gonzalez J, Gulbrandsen M. Innovation in established industries undergoing digital transformation: The role of collective identity and public values. Innovation 2022; 24(1): 201-30.
[http://dx.doi.org/10.1080/14479338.2021.1938578]

[42]   Srinidhi NN, Kumar SMD, Venugopal KR. Network optimizations in the Internet of Things: A review. Eng Sci Technol 2019; 22(1): 1-21.

[http://dx.doi.org/10.1016/j.jestch.2018.09.003]

[43]   Thiyam. (n.d.). The_need_for_digitization.

[44]   Udovita PVMVD. Conceptual review on dimensions of digital transformation in modern era. Int J Sci Res 2020; 10(2): p9873.
[http://dx.doi.org/10.29322/IJSRP.10.02.2020.p9873]

[45]   Venkatesh R, Mathew L, Singhal TK. Imperatives of business models and digital transformation for digital services providers. Int J Bus Data Commun Networking 2019; 15(1): 105-24.
[http://dx.doi.org/10.4018/IJBDCN.2019010107]

[46]   Verhoef PC, Broekhuizen T, Bart Y, *et al.* Digital transformation: A multidisciplinary reflection and research agenda. J Bus Res 2021; 122: 889-901.
[http://dx.doi.org/10.1016/j.jbusres.2019.09.022]

[47]   Vogelsang K, Liere-Netheler K, Packmohr S, Hoppe U. Success factors for fostering a digital transformation in manufacturing companies. J Enterp Transform 2018; 8(1-2): 121-42.
[http://dx.doi.org/10.1080/19488289.2019.1578839]

[48]   Wahyu Wasono Mihardjo L, Sasmoko S. Digital Transformation: Digital Leadership Role in Developing Business Model Innovation Mediated by Co-Creation Strategy for Telecommunication Incumbent Firms. Strategy and Behaviors in the Digital Economy 2020.
[http://dx.doi.org/10.5772/intechopen.82517]

[49]   Ware C. Foundations for an applied science of data visualization. Information Visualization. 2013; pp. 1-30.
[http://dx.doi.org/10.1016/B978-0-12-381464-7.00001-6]

[50]   Waskom M. seaborn: Statistical data visualization. J Open Source Softw 2021; 6(60): 3021.
[http://dx.doi.org/10.21105/joss.03021]

[51]   Woodside JM, Florea M. Security intelligence for healthcare mobile electronic commerce. Security intelligence for healthcare mobile electronic commerce. 1st Ed.., CRC Press 2014.
[http://dx.doi.org/10.1201/b17686-19]

[52]   World Economic Forum. The Impact of 5G: Creating New Value across Industries and Society. 2020. Available from: http://www3.weforum.org/docs/WEF_The_Impact_of_5G_Report.pdf

[53]   Adapting to the digital trade era : challenges and opportunities 2021. Available from: https://www.wto.org/english/res_e/booksp_e/adtera_e.pdf

[54]   Ziyadin S, Suieubayeva S, Utegenova A. Digital transformation in business.Digital Age: Chances, Challenges and Future. 2020; pp. 408-15.
[http://dx.doi.org/10.1007/978-3-030-27015-5_49]

CHAPTER 7

The Role of Social Media as a Promotional Tool for SMEs in Ghana

Kobby Mensah[1,*], Stephen Mahama Braimah[1], Awini Gideon[2] and Zakari Bukari[3]

[1] *University of Ghana, Legon-Ghana*

[2] *Department of Marketing, Tamale Technical University, Tamale-Ghana*

[3] *University of Professional Studies, Accra-Ghana*

Abstract: This study aims to investigate how social media functions as a marketing tool for SMEs in Ghana. An unstructured and semi-structured interview guide was employed, and a qualitative research methodology was applied. The responses from twenty respondents from a few chosen SMEs in the Greater Accra area formed the basis of the analysis. Ghanaian SMEs have the chance to invest in their social media marketing and create more targeted campaigns. They can also utilize the platform to promote direct sales, acquire an understanding of how customers view and value a brand, and achieve lifetime value targets like client acquisition and retention. The study revealed that SMEs in Ghana mostly use Facebook, Instagram, YouTube, Twitter, and LinkedIn as their social media platforms. The report also suggests that media organizations create a content roadmap to ensure that their material is designed with social media interaction in mind, such as the usage of extremely brief videos and ephemeral content, to maximize their desired earned media engagement.

Keywords: Blogging, Entrepreneur, Ghana, Social Media, SMEs.

INTRODUCTION

Many people have been able to pursue self-employment because of the growth of social media, thanks to the numerous options and low barriers to entry. The growth of social media has enabled many to pursue self-employment due to its multiple options and easy entry. The majority of business owners have largely relied on social media sites like YouTube, Instagram, Twitter, Facebook, *etc* [1]. to share content and market their products [2]. Women are the majority of social media influencers worldwide, making up around 77 percent of all influencers.

* **Corresponding author Kobby Mensah:** University of Ghana, Legon-Ghana; E-mail:kobbymensah@ug.edu.gh

Mohammed Majeed, Abdul-Razak Abubakari, Awini Gideon and Jayadatta S. (Eds.)

They take advantage of this by starting their own businesses. Similar to this, both men and women use the rise of social media to launch their own enterprises. Entrepreneurs are using social media platforms more and more to advertise their businesses, as well as for marketing and building client relationships [3, 4]. According to Datta *et al.* [1], social media has given business owners more opportunities to interact with people. Thus, entrepreneurs can build ties with customers or other business owners using social media. In addition to increasing visibility, social media has boosted client interactions through advertising, endorsements, and other business-related activities, which has helped businesses increase their sales. Additionally, social media has given business owners the tools they need to track rivals and promote anywhere in the world. One of the best tools for organizations to use for advertising or promotion is social media. Entrepreneurs can monitor and stay informed about their potential clients and/or business opportunities thanks to social media. Furthermore, business owners can use social media to manage and strengthen their offline and online relationships [5]. Ghanaian business people have benefited from the emergence of social media to promote and publicize their goods and/or services. Youth in Ghana make up the majority of the population; they tend to be more business-and tech-savvy. Social media is also extensively used by event management businesses in Accra, including Lionheart events, Ark event management services, Geovision services, Charterhouse event organizers, *etc.*

That said, the emergence of social media has presented a challenge to businesses as they struggle to create an SM community and formulate a strategy. The majority of businesses use social media without realizing its influence, strength, and virility [30]. In spite of the immense advantages that social media (SM) offers to business owners, relatively few do so in sub-Saharan Africa. If small and medium-sized businesses (SMEs) can take advantage of the benefits that SM provides, they stand to benefit and grow exponentially. Regardless of social media's significance and power, the majority of organizations still lack a focused social media strategy. Organizations frequently experience confusion when deploying SM tactics. Due to the fact that users are no longer naive, social media has created bottlenecks and opportunities for brands [6]. The use of social media has become increasingly important in promoting businesses to a target audience. Anecdotal evidence reveals that most organizations overlook this clarion call when implementing SM strategies. This study investigates how small and medium enterprises (SMEs) can capitalize on the benefits that social media presents. "How SMEs may overcome the hurdles of using social media to promote their business" is the focus of the study. The research's primary objective is to: 1. Examine whether event management companies advertise on social media. 2. To examine the difficulties SME's encounter while utilizing social media to market their businesses. 3. Outlining solutions to discovered problems.

Following the research's historical context, this study is organized to provide context for the aforementioned subject. First and foremost, section 2 would include a review of the existing literature that explicitly articulates all relevant concepts and theories underlying the investigation. Moving on, section 3 describes the methods and strategy used by the researcher. In section 4, the research provides its findings and discusses them, followed by a review of the literature and a summary. Section 5 concludes by presenting the findings, drawing further conclusions, and offering suggestions for additional research.

LITERATURE METHODOLOGY

Peer reviewed open access publications from journals included in the "observatory of international research" (OOIR) and the "academy of journal guide list" (CABS list) were chosen. To make the current research agenda obvious, "key topics, arguments, and developments in the literature over time with the concepts, theories, and empirical data advanced were analyzed."

Concept and Definitions of Social Media

Over the years, social media as an idea has experienced numerous transformations. Social media are websites used for social networking and blogging, according to the Merriam-Webster Dictionary. To share information, ideas, personal messages, and other stuff, users establish online communities (such as videos). The internet is necessary for social media to work effectively. According to Kaplan & Haelein [7], the definition should be focused on "user-generated content" and "Web 2.0." Richter and Koch [8] further defined social media as all online tools, media, and platforms that facilitate content exchange and communication on a worldwide scale. Social media applications do not just include Facebook, Instagram, Twitter, Snapchat, Hike, Flickr, "Yahoo, Skype, Imo, Myspace, BBM, Viber, and WhatsApp" [9]. According to studies on users' favourite social networking platforms, WhatsApp continues to be the most widely used social media program.

The five primary categories of social media are "social networking sites (SNS)," media sharing websites, blogs, microblogging, and social news. For instance, social media can be divided into media web applications; microblogs as a platform for sharing media; and blogs as a platform for dissemination of media.

Traditional Media and Digital Media

Digital media are modern forms of communication that encourage user-generated content and active participation. It is communication that takes place over digital platforms, including social media, the web, and mobile phones. It also entails the creation of mobile applications with notification features that inform consumers of newly published news that is current. Print and electronic media are both part of traditional media. All forms of media that are not web-based are included, including print and electronic media like radio and television. "About 72 percent of the Ghanaian population rely on and trust social media information, and hence its usage for business transactions, as SM is now seen as a medium for advertising goods and services. This has really accrued to the revenue base of SM (see Table 2)," according to the Afro Barometer [10]. Ads from public and private organisations are the traditional media's primary source of income. The expansion and effectiveness of conventional media are hampered by their excessive reliance on advertising income to cover their operating costs. Consumers pay the normal price, which is why businesses use conventional advertising channels. Despite these changes, Ghana has had strong growth trends in traditional media over the past 20 years, notably in the West African nation.

Table 1. Social Media App Type of social media regularly used.

Social Media	Percent
WhatsApp	83.3
Facebook	78.0
Twitter	12.8
LinkedIn	7.9
Instagram	7.5
Imo	2.6
Snapchat	1.8
MySpace	1.3
Skype	0.9
GOAT	0.4
Badoo	0.4
YouTube	0.4
WeChat	0.4
Total	100.0

Source: Adapted from Akakandelwa & Walubita [11]

Table 2. Social media revenue in ghana.

Social Media (SM) Platforms	Revenue (in percent)
Facebook	58.55%
Twitter	21.52%

(Table 2) cont.....

Social Media (SM) Platforms	Revenue (in percent)
Pinterest	13.73%
YouTube	4.91%
Instagram	0.94%
LinkedIn	0.12%

Source: Statcounter [12].

A range of highly targeted, defined, and specialized media are replacing traditional mass media advertising to engage different client segments with more individualized and interactive content [13]. The new media include blogs, online advertisements, made-for-the-web videos, specialty cable channels like DSTV and GOTV, as well as an increasing number of social media websites. The key is to combine all of these media in a way that best engages consumers and raises brand preference for the medium.

Media Channels

A media channel is a platform or a medium through which a sender's encoded message is transmitted to a receiver [14]. Traditional and digital media channels are among them, but they are not the only ones. Examples were given in the earlier section of the body (see Table **1**). Table **3** below provides more information and examples to further highlight the differences.

Table 3. Traditional and digital media channels.

Traditional Media Channels	Digital Media Channels
Television	Online channels such as websites.
Radio	Mobile- mobile applications and USSD codes.
Print media channels- newspapers, magazines,	Social Media Channels- Facebook, Twitter, Instagram, YouTube *etc.*

Source: Statcounter [12].

Social Media Advertising

Social media, as generally described by Kaplan and Haenlein [7], is a collection of web-based programs that enable the production and sharing of user-generated content. Twitter, Facebook, and WhatsApp are examples of social networking and microblogging websites. Snapchat is a picture messaging app, while Instagram is a normal photo and video-sharing platform. Kotler [15], defines advertising as "any paid form of non-personal presentation and promotion of ideas, goods, or services by an identified sponsor" (p. 19). Therefore, social media advertising is the impersonal presentation of concepts, products, or services on social media by a designated sponsor. The decision typically depends on the goals and results the sponsor is trying to achieve. "The sponsor may limit the advertisement to just one social media platform or use a combination of several" [16].

Over time, social media advertising has changed. Influencer marketing advertising is another name for the type of social media advertising known as influencer advertising. Influencer marketing is inherently a potent source of eWOM that lends some creativity and authenticity to company advertisements on social media. Previous studies have provided empirical support for the use of influencers such as celebrities and bloggers to dramatically affect consumer attitudes and purchase intentions [17, 18]. In order to market their products, businesses have turned to and invested in social media (SM) advertising on sites like Facebook, Instagram, and Twitter [19]. The exciting feature of "social media advertising" that sets it out favourably from "traditional media advertising" is the range of customer interaction choices it provides. Social media advertising stands out from "traditional media advertising" due to its broader customer interaction options.

Social Media Content

Well-crafted content increases traffic and engagement for businesses that rely on social media to conduct business. Without content, social media marketing cannot work effectively [13]. Content marketing is a strategic marketing strategy that focuses on producing and disseminating useful, pertinent, and consistent content, according to the Content Marketing Institute. The goal of "content marketing" is to provide customers with constant, worthwhile information in order to increase traffic and engagement, which will eventually lead to profitable customer behavior. Consumers that actively share and interact with brands on social media about relevant topics are engaging in content marketing. The three basic categories of social media content marketing are rational (also known as "informational, functional, educational, or current event), interactional (*e.g.*, personal, employee, brand community, customer connection, and cause-related), and transactional (referring to remunerative, brand resonance, and sales promotion)." Social media content's impact on engagement has been a topic of discussion for some time. Coelho, Oliveira, and Almeida [20] found no evidence of a connection between interaction on Facebook and Instagram and the impact of reasonable material. According to Cvijikj and Michahelles [21], likes and comments provide empirical evidence. Likes are a sort of passive participation, while more active engagement is not influenced by rational content (such as comments). Customers favor using and engaging with a company's social media. Organizations capitalize on this opportunity by creating social media content that appeals to and engages their target audience.

Small and Medium Enterprises (SMEs) and Social Media Usage

In contrast to other marketing techniques, social media marketing provides a number of tools that are very simple to use and are completely free. Amplification of word-of-mouth marketing, market research, general marketing, idea generation, and new product development are the justifications for employing social media marketing. Facebook usage among SMEs aids numerous businesses in achieving their organizational goals, including those related to marketing, communication, sales, advertising, innovation, problem-solving, customer service, human resources, information technology, and promoting cultural change. Internet-enabled communication tools enable businesses to conduct transactions anytime, anywhere. Small and medium-sized businesses (SMEs) use Facebook and other "social media platforms" to interact with "customers" and foster internal communication and collaboration. Adoption of social media is influenced by variables like compatibility, affordability, trust, interaction, and interactivity. If social media platforms offer a sizable amount of timely, relevant, high-quality content, SMEs will use them.

Theoretical Background

Uses and Gratification Theory

The essay "on the use of mass media for vital things" is where the uses and gratification theory first emerged (see [22]). The phrase "UG theory" has now developed beyond its original context and is used in a wide range of disciplines. The UG theory is a method for comprehending how people actively seek out particular media, communicate with one another, and consume content. Peirce [23] claims that in order to satisfy the demands of the audience, pleasure comprises motives including "cognitive needs, affective needs, and social integrative needs." However, the fundamental idea of use and pleasure is simple; it involves normative influences, societal changes, and people's responses to the status of society. When it comes to how organizations employ the drivers of relationships to accomplish organizational goals, relationships are a key element of use and pleasure. Key motivators for group actions in communication and public relations include media content, exposure, and the social environment [23, 24]. Businesses can use drivers of media satisfaction to connect with customers by building relationships or engaging with them. Customers can discover specific details about other connections' histories, music tastes, interests, and whereabouts through social media.

Uses and Gratification and Social Media

A component of the UG theory is observing how and why people actively seek out particular media for specific purposes . The functionalist paradigm of social science, which focuses on the investigation of uses and gratification, has replaced the outdated media impact in the majority of studies. According to Awini [25], every medium for mass engagement offers an advanced way at the beginning. SM is being used to maintain long-distance relationships. Having said that, technology like distribution lists, search engines, and photo directories may help maintain online relationships. According to Thompson *et al.* [26], social media enables users to communicate with one another in a variety of ways within the platform, including through chat, private messages, tweets, retweets, links to external information, and the sharing of images and videos. These requirements, which cause reasons to vary, depend on social networking sites' features and nature.

Social media platforms might help in the creation of an online networking community for individuals who present themselves to revitalize deep-rooted affiliations and create new affiliations. Ellison *et al.* [27] stated that social networking sites are concerned with work-related contexts such as keeping others informed about such things as music, politics, products or services. Social media relationships and participation are growing. Online users are at a disadvantage since they are excluded from the expansion of relationships and pleasures. Utilization and satisfaction act as a facilitator for people to develop and manage the information flowing in a relationship [28]. According to Shao [29], social media could significantly boost participation because the technology is perfectly adapted to maintain these relationships affordably and easily. Social media use and gratification have an impact on an organization's performance, which explains how much a company nurtures and develops relationships with its clients.

SMEs may openly connect and build relationships with potential customers thanks to the personal disclosure and interactive tools on SM. The information offered on social media platforms may provide a hint as to how to engage users; therefore, it may be based on natural page interactions. Additionally, it might assist SMEs in locating potential clients about whom they are unaware. Because consumer engagement is a significant benefit that results from social media activities, SMEs and marketing people can increase their involvement by utilizing social media. It is widely acknowledged that customer involvement is precisely and unmistakably linked to a number of outcomes, including trust, fulfillment, duty, and loyalty [30, 31].

Theoretical Framework

Approximately forty-three percent (43%) of the 24 publications under consideration had no clearly indicated theoretical backing, which means that these investigations did not explicitly refer to any particular theory. The study's findings are consistent with those of Knoll [32], who stated clearly that 45% of the publications he assessed lacked a specific theoretical foundation. Socialization theory, social comparison theory, uses and gratification theory, and social identity theory were all mentioned extensively in research works that included a theoretical framework. The creation and exchange of content by users on SM are linked to the possibility of users influencing one another through pre-existing connections [7]. Users on SM create and share content, potentially influencing each other through existing connections. Some studies have been successful in fusing marketing theory with theories from other disciplines, such as "customer value theory" [33] and the "hierarchy of effects" (HOE) model [34]. The social capital hypothesis, which emphasized the social networks theory, was also used in several studies. The concept cannot be adequately addressed by a single theory due to the dynamic nature and variety of social media. Multiple theories have been utilized in some studies [35] to explain how people use social media.

Conceptual Framework

The conceptual framework demonstrates the relationship between the study's research questions and its research purpose. The researchers created a conceptual framework outlining the relationship between the independent variables that have an impact on the performance of SMEs based on the review of the literature. The framework's main elements function separately from one another. The concept demonstrates how social media participation has an interactive impact on SMEs' customer loyalty and, consequently, performance. The conceptual structure of this study is depicted in Fig. (**1**) below, where social media activity acts as a mediator between the dependent variable and its antecedent.

METHODOLOGY

The segment provides a detailed explanation of the approach taken to address the study's objectives.

Empirical Context

We conducted a study in Ghana, a country with a developing economy. The responders were also staff members or workers of some selected Ghanaian SMEs. However, their knowledge and focus allowed them to provide a greater range of real-world examples. Because of our choice of context, we were able to have a sample control.

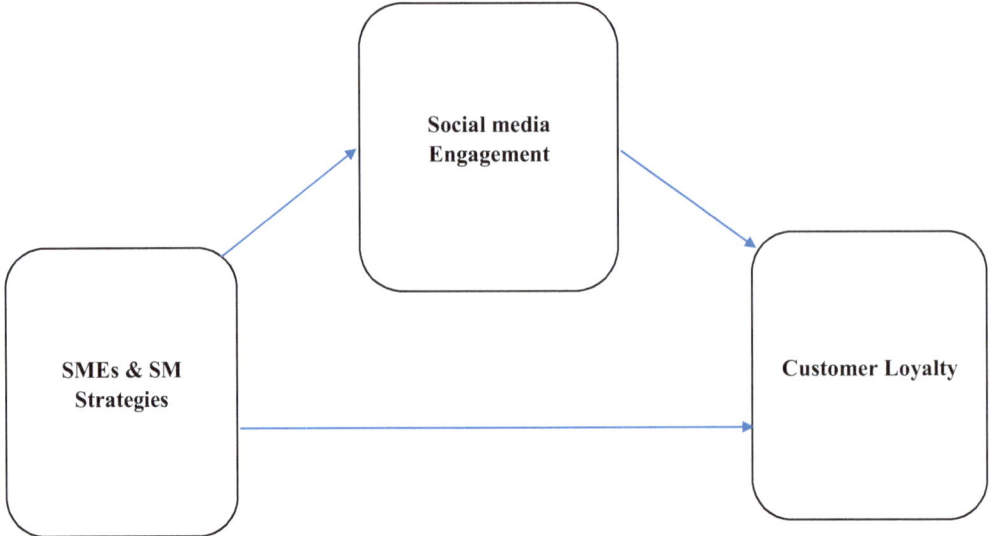

Fig. (1). Conceptual framework.

Data Collection Techniques

The phenomenon of social media (SM) as a promotional tool for SMEs in Ghana was examined using in-depth interviews. This approach aims to accurately represent the participant's viewpoint on a study problem. Boyce and Neale [36] claim that this approach provides "much more detailed information" than surveys. The survey had 65 participants from Ghanaian SMEs. The participants posed a number of questions regarding SM and its impact on business performance. Only 20 people were picked for the interview due to their exceptional SM knowledge. For the investigation, interviewees were given pseudonyms ranging from R1 to R20. With the participants' permission, all of the interviews were recorded.

Data Analysis

In addition to recording and transcribing the interviews, human coding was employed to enhance, condense, and organize the data into themes. Individual responses were integrated using cross-case analysis to test the comparability of responses until all new units could be maintained in the appropriate category, as advised by Flick [37].

RESULTS AND FINDINGS

The results of the studies were arranged and presented based on the primary and subthemes identified in the empirical data.

What is your Understanding of Social Media Content and its Relevance to SMEs?

"Social Media Content simply refers to information that individual or business publish on their social media channels, this can be informed of infographics, textual and other formats, Content created to be consumed through social channels and also, Social Media is an essential to my organization due the fact that, it offers us the opportunity connects with customers across the globe and also help us to get live feedbacks from customers which help us to improve upon our products and services" (Respondent 1).

"It's any idea that's visualized with the aim of promoting, broadcasting, educating or provision of service. It comes in many forms. It could be graphic, video, sound or animation. Whereas, with social media, we're able to target potential clients by letting them know the services we provide. Our social media contents are also our portfolio" (Respondent 3).

"Social media content is strategic ideas put together to engage followers and well I worked in the marketing and advertising space for social media content helps to reach out on what we do across the world" (Respondent 5).

"It can be informative, educative or entertainment content to enable your audience understand more of your brand and its equally relevant to an organisation because every other information is easily accessible to all" (Respondent 7).

"Social media content contains information regarding a company or a product that's directed to customers or potential clients and also, social media content is very important to all organisations because it will help in engaging consumers and creating traffic for the organisation" (Respondent 8).

"Social media content is an information that is being given out for formal and informal purposes the message shown to promote a product or business. It is important because, it helps institutions to create the aware of their brand and this can lead to brand loyalty" (Respondent 11).

"Content is the total understanding of a product or service broken-down into pieces for consumer to understand and its relevant because it helps in our day-to-day operations and engagement with the general public" (Respondent 12).

"Social media content contains everything from entertainment, health, business, education etc. it is also relevant to business by creating leads and increasing the sales volume of the organisation" (Respondent 13).

"Social media content is about ideas and thoughts displayed through various forms on social media. It is equally relevant to organisations because it's the very bedrock of communicating with customers" (Respondent 15).

"Social media content includes posts from individuals or companies in reaching their target audience with a product or service. It is our best way of showcasing our goods and services to a wider market. It's the way I get to keep my customers active and informed about me and my services. Also, my organisation only uses social media to attract future employees and it keeps one updated on current trends" (Respondent 17).

Social media content assists SMEs in increasing sales value, building brand awareness and loyalty, as well as engaging users and driving traffic that results in the purchase of goods and/or services. Surprisingly, the purpose of "content marketing" is to provide customers with constant, useful material in order to increase traffic and engagement. A multi-channel strategy is used by businesses to generate earned social media as a result of the development of social media, which has encouraged social methods in the form of "electronic word of mouth" (eWOM). Customers create earned social media independently of the business in a variety of ways, from "paid and owned media."

How do you Utilize Social Media Content in Marketing your Firm and how does Social Media Content Influence the Choice of your Products?

Social media aids SMEs in posting content and interacting with customers in an effort to increase interest in the company's goods and/or services. Additionally, it aids in raising awareness of a company's goods and services as well as any pertinent qualities. Utilizing social media material aids in the organization's strategic positioning. According to those who participated in the interviews, social media content provides a precise understanding of the goods and services that the SME offers. "Social media content helps me identify what's relevant and vice versa, concerns emerging from the aforementioned firm," one interviewee remarked. The selection of a product or service is also influenced by social media content. According to a recent poll by the Ghanaian Chamber of Commerce and Industry, Ghanaian SMEs are not using social media as effectively as foreign businesses (GCCI). Increased traffic from social media might result in increased user engagement.

How can you Leverage on Social Media to Promote or Market your Product or Services?

"Social Media can be used to used promote or market businesses by targeting user class relevant to your business and serving them with the relevant content" (Respondent 1).

"Getting to know your target audience listening to questions being asked in various niche related spaces and crating content to answer those questions and put out meaningful content they can relate to" (Respondent 4).

"Majority of Ghanaians are on one social platform or the other. This makes it easier to sell based on where the target audience are and this serves as an avenue to promote organisatin's goods and services" (Respondent 7).

"It helps you define your target market and try connecting to that demographic on whichever social media platforms they are most likely to be on" (Respondent 8).

"Social media as a promotional tool is putting together the right content for the right audience and keeping up with trends cleverly intertwining them with your message and product" (Respondent 11).

The use of "social media as a marketing" technique aids in the development of an organization's goods and/or services. Influencer marketing refers to the process of finding and exploiting these social media resources to promote a business on social media. Social media can inherently be used as a potent eWOM source or marketing tool.

Do you Benefit using Social Media to Promote your Product/Services?

According to anecdotal evidence from the field and respondents' viewpoints, social networking is advantageous for businesses that use these digital technologies. Social media facilitates improved customer communication, the spread of information, and the generation of leads that ultimately lead to increased sales. SMEs require social media for increased sales volume, customer loyalty, brand awareness, competitive edge, *etc*. Social media may aid SMEs in increasing sales, but it also draws in new clients, gathers their opinions, and fosters a sense of loyalty. According to one respondent, "it doesn't cost me anything to put it online using social media."

What are some of the Challenges of Social Media Advertising?

Seventy-five percent (75%) of the twenty respondents—15 out of them—have talked about or made reference to the difficulties or blockages in social media advertising. These respondents identified and discussed a few of the difficulties that "social media advertising" in Ghana may face. The opinions of the respondents on the difficulties of "social media advertising" are shown below.

"Some of the challenges affect our business in the following ways. 1. Low Sales. 2. Not getting the right feedback from customers" (Respondent 1).

"You might miss your target audience which in turn, decreases sales" (Respondent 4).

"People who have a bad experience makes it difficult for genuine businesses when they are transacting with the firm on social media" (Respondent 5).

"It is costly when brand influencers get involved" (Respondent 10).

"Followers are conversations that are often faked by a biased group of hired followers thereby causing the brand or business to lose out on valuable and authentic conversations" (Respondent 11).

"Conversations generated from social media when not managed well could lead to a potential crisis. As followers of influencing may interpret posts in a way that demean brand image" (Respondent 12).

"Brands do not have control over the way and extent to which social media advertising is put out. It can sometimes be mistaken as paid and create an impression of the brand not being transparent" (Respondent 13).

"A challenge can be with the content itself not generating any leads through social media" (Respondent 15).

"There are numerous challenges facing social media advertising and these include; increasing ad cost, declining organic reach and engagement cost, identifying the right platform for the audience, understanding the target audience and defining the marketing goal" (Respondent 16).

Some of the difficulties Ghanaian SMEs encounter while using social media for advertising include a decline in sales as a result of bad virility and the need to use paid advertisements in order to reach more people. Some of the respondents also described some of the SMEs' social media marketing difficulties. It is crucial to filter individuals on social media to discover the correct clients because not all of them are interested in your goods or services. One respondent stated that "deceptive sales of things leaves people not having too much faith in doing online business because there are many scammers out there," one respondent stated. The study will assist businesses in devising measures to relieve bottlenecks and increase their ability to compete with their fiercest rivals.

How does the Challenges of Social Media Advertisement Affect your Firm?

"Loss of revenue due to inability to monetize their social media value" (Respondent 1).

"Gradual loss of influence to new media entities and bloggers. Losing touch of news generation of audiences (generation Z and C) who are social media heavy" (Respondent 2).

"Can be misleading at times that what worked or did not work for some small number of persons will apply to all Can tarnish the reputation of brands when negative WOM about a brand goes out" (Respondent 3).

"While social media gives you the chance to build brand awareness and customer loyalty, there are also dangers in participating in a public conversation forum. You need to have a clear idea of how to handle negative feedback about your business. You need to ensure that what you post and how you interact with people presents a professional image to the world. Writing down a set of rules for how you will manage social media can help you to steer through the challenges" (Respondent 5).

"It affects their revenue especially when a competitor surfaces. If they do not make use of the earned content for brands on social media, the news media firms will suffer big time" (Respondent 6).

Case 8 *"Finding the right customers class for the business. Numbers on social media not translating into sales"* (Respondent 8).

"Putting out financial content in a fun way a lot of ppl can interact with" (Respondent 10).

"Since the steps to creating promotions vary from platform to platform, it's quite difficult remembering and following each step every time. It would be much helpful if all social media platforms had a specific keyword or questions which would mean one has to learn the steps once" (Respondent 13).

The respondents also discussed some of the issues SMEs face with "social media advertising" and how it may negatively impact SMEs. These negative effects were listed as follows: a sharp decline in the firm's revenue as a result of the firm's sales volume; the potential for bad press or brand image; an impact on the organization's customer base; the potential for the firm to stray from its target audience; and the potential for a high rate of customer churn. The interviewees stated that if caution is not taken, the difficulties outlined will significantly impact SMEs and will likely lead to customer churn and appalling performance of the business.

In your Opinion what are some of Solutions to Curb these Challenges?

Eighty percent (80%) of the respondents have talked about or highlighted potential solutions to the problems or bottlenecks that "social media advertising" in Ghana faces.

"Not only will a social media strategy help to keep you on track, it will also allow you to measure how you're doing. When defining your strategy, it's a good time to choose which metrics you're going to monitor. These are things I do and it does influence the objectives I have" (Respondent 2).

"Defining quantifiable goals allows you to attach a number to them so they can be tracked. For example, this could include app downloads, purchases, newsletter sign-ups or gated content downloads. In order to track your performance with accuracy, I always monitor the page engagement, sales, referral traffic, bounce rate, and return on ad spend, and this has been fantastic since" (Respondent 3).

"One way to remain up to date is to subscribe to reputable sources and publications to receive the latest news and announcements. As cliché as it sounds, it's crucial to carve some time out to keep learning – it will bring huge benefits to your marketing efforts and helps keep those creative juices flowing too" (Respondent 4).

"To me, one way to curb these challenges is to improve our social media engagement. Engagement is a significant part of social media marketing. It's more than just a metric to measure effectiveness, and its equally good to engage with your audience, tag other accounts in your posts, usage of pertinent hashtags and as well encouraging user generated content (UGC)" (Respondent 5).

"Growing your social following fits hand in hand with growing your engagement. The more people you reach, the more people discover your brand and the more likely they are to follow and engage with you" (Respondent 7).

"Building an authentic connection with your prospective customers is key and one way is to reply their comments with a personal response, asking your audience questions that are relevant to them, respond to negative feedback as well as positive to make them feel valued, and I show them how you are listening to them" (Respondent 8).

"Many social media platforms revolve around visual content and great visual content can make you stand out on the feed. It takes time and skill to create imagery and videos that really work" (Respondent 9).

"Assess your top-performing posts to understand what drives the most interactions. Try to find common threads between these posts (think: timing, content themes, post types, formatting, voice)" (Respondent 10).

"Focus on content that taps into your existing followers, customers and community. This might include question-based content, user-generated content campaigns and responding to shout-outs and comments" (Respondent 11).

"Consider collaborating with influencers and brands as a way to extend your reach and encourage more brand mentions" (Respondent 12).

"Developing a distinct brand voice, don't discount the power of personality (think: humor, relatability) as a way to stand out" (Respondent 13).

"I always activate my to boost my brand's content and reach beyond our own account" (Respondent 14).

"Consider outsourcing or sharing responsibilities across your marketing team as needed" (Respondent 16).

"Define your "priority" network and focus most of your efforts there. Ask yourself: where do you have the most meaningful interaction? Where are you seeing the most growth? Which platform is tied most to your business goals?" (Respondent 17).

"Always assess your CRM data to better understand how your company's social presence impacts your marketing and sales funnel" (Respondent 19).

"Remember to discuss goals and expectations with your managers and higher-ups to make sure everyone is on the same page. Double-check that you're focusing on the appropriate metrics and KPIs" (Respondent 20).

Since the majority of SMEs are "ponzi schemes," SMEs need to build trust with their audience. To do this, they must develop a "social media marketing plan." In addition to consistently producing high-quality and interesting content, training your team or employees is crucial to fixing the problems. According to the American Customer Satisfaction Index (CVI), a gauge of satisfaction with the customer service provided by major chains like Starbucks, Kia Motors, and McDonald's, when customers are well engaged and served with superior customer service, it will go a long way to result in customer loyalty.

DISCUSSION AND FINDINGS

The goal of content marketing is to provide customers with constant, worthwhile information in order to increase traffic and engagement, which will eventually lead to profitable customer behavior. The comments of the respondents revealed that social media content assists SMEs in increasing their sales value. According to the respondents, traditional media outlets were the only ones who could employ earned social media in the past. However, the emergence of "social media, which allows user-generated content, has facilitated social approaches in the form of electronic word of mouth (eWOM)." The majority of participants agreed that social media content promotes SMEs. It was discovered that social media presents a wealth of options for both consumers and businesses, notwithstanding the constraints. Social media has given customers new methods to communicate with brands. Businesses have the chance to spend money on their social media presence and create more specialized campaigns. The fact that "social media marketing is highly associated with advertising and its potential for boosting business and executing promotional activities to reach and communicate with targeted clients" is noteworthy [3].

SME bottlenecks might include, but are not limited to: declining revenues as a result of bad virility; needing to run paid advertisements to attract a larger audience. This is because social media has a large user base, some of whom utilize it for a variety of reasons. It's crucial to filter users on social media to locate the proper clients for your company because not all users are interested in your goods or services. One respondent stated that "deceptive sales of things leaves people not having too much faith in doing online business because there are many scammers out there," one respondent stated. The study will assist businesses in devising measures to relieve bottlenecks and increase their ability to compete with their fiercest rivals.

According to a poll conducted by the Association of Small and Medium Enterprises (ASME), Ghanaian SMEs are using Facebook, Instagram, YouTube, Twitter, and LinkedIn to connect with their target market. An ASME survey found that in Ghana, SMEs most frequently used social media channels. Regarding the solutions, it was found in the study that since the majority of SMEs in Ghana are "ponzi schemes," they must build trust with their audience. Additionally, developing a social media marketing strategy is crucial for SMEs in limiting bottlenecks; training your team or staff is equally important in resolving the challenges; posting quality and engaging content consistently is key; and creating quality visuals is also important. By exposing these countermeasures, SMEs will become more visible and productive because their materials will attract interest, which will result in sales.

CONCLUSION

Existing media practices have evolved as a result of the arrival of new communication platforms like Facebook, Instagram, Twitter, and LinkedIn. SME media engagements and practices are no longer limited to their various print and electronic media. The proliferation of smartphones, the growth of the internet, and the uptake of these new media outlets have all had an impact on how audiences have converged on these platforms [38]. Small and medium-sized enterprises (SMEs) in Ghana have quickly adapted to new media trends and now have blogs and pages on the various media platforms where news is created and shared. Because of this, social media is beginning to supplant traditional media as the preferred platform for many SMEs. Because social media is now viewed as a means of advertising goods and services, the Afro Barometer [10] revealed that 72% of Ghanaians rely on and trust social media information. As a result, social media is now used for business transactions, which has significantly increased the revenue base of SMEs. The study also showed that conventional media includes radio, television, newspapers, and other print media. The editorial teams and managers of these media outlets are primarily responsible for creating the program line-ups, which are the content of the media. To cover its operating costs, India's traditional media mainly relies on advertising revenue. Due to the high advertising expenses involved with TV advertising, SMEs that use traditional advertising mediums are at a severe disadvantage as the cost is typically passed on to consumers [39].

RECOMMENDATION

The following actions have been advised following a thorough analysis of the results and conclusion:

SMEs should invest in training employees who can promote their companies on social media. Refresher training must be organized so that employees have the knowledge and abilities to increase business for the company and generate income.

Thus, they should engage specialists in social media and digital marketing to assist in identifying the value of social media for SMEs in Ghana.

The health of the company's social media efforts should be evaluated by the SMEs using analytical hooks, tools, and toolkits.

They should create a content roadmap to ensure that the material is intended for social media platforms in order to maximize the social media interaction they require, such as using very short videos and transient content.

LIMITATION AND FUTURE RESEARCH

In around sixteen (16) of Ghana's regions, there are SMEs. However, this study only looked at respondents from the Greater Accra region. The study's findings might not necessarily apply to other SMEs in Ghana that use or consume social media. The study's results are also restricted to SMEs in Ghana's Greater Accra region and may not necessarily be extrapolated to other SMEs in the country's other regions, making the sample size somewhat small. As a result, the study's geographic scope is restricted to Ghana, and it may not be applicable to other nations on the list.

FUTURE STUDIES

Future research should examine the function of earned social media advertising in Ghana's competitive markets, according to the study's recommendations. Future studies should take into account how sales in Ghana are impacted by traditional and social media. In order to quantify the elements that generate income for firms in Ghana and for the results to be more generally applicable, future studies should take "into account the importance of social media advertising in Ghana" as well as adopt a bigger sample size utilizing a quantitative approach.

REFERENCES

[1]　Datta KS, Adkins O, Fitzsimmons JR. Entrepreneurship and social media influencers in an Islamic context. Understanding Social Media and Entrepreneurship. Cham: Springer 2020; pp. 121-39.
[http://dx.doi.org/10.1007/978-3-030-43453-3_7]

[2]　Troise C, Dana LP, Tani M, Lee KY. Social media and entrepreneurship: exploring the impact of social media use of start-ups on their entrepreneurial orientation and opportunities. J Small Bus Enterprise Dev 2021.

[3]　Alalwan AA, Rana NP, Dwivedi YK, Algharabat R. Social media in marketing: A review and analysis of the existing literature. Telemat Inform 2017; 34(7): 1177-90.
[http://dx.doi.org/10.1016/j.tele.2017.05.008]

[4]　Misirlis N, Vlachopoulou M. Social media metrics and analytics in marketing – S3M: A mapping literature review. Int J Inf Manage 2018; 38(1): 270-6.
[http://dx.doi.org/10.1016/j.ijinfomgt.2017.10.005]

[5]　Wang W, Liang Q, Mahto RV, Deng W, Zhang SX. Entrepreneurial entry: The role of social media. Technol Forecast Soc Change 2020; 161: 120337.
[http://dx.doi.org/10.1016/j.techfore.2020.120337] [PMID: 33012851]

[6]　Jin SAA, Phua J. Following celebrities' tweets about brands: The impact of twitter-based electronic word-of-mouth on consumers' source credibility perception, buying intention, and social identification with celebrities. J Advert 2014; 43(2): 181-95.
[http://dx.doi.org/10.1080/00913367.2013.827606]

[7]　Richter A, Koch M. Functions of social networking services. From CSCW to Web 2.0. European Developments in Collaborative Design Selected Papers from COOP08 2008.

[8]　Eid MIM, Al-Jabri IM. Social networking, knowledge sharing, and student learning: The case of university students. Comput Educ 2016; 99: 14-27.

[http://dx.doi.org/10.1016/j.compedu.2016.04.007]

[9]   Afro Barometer. Available From: https://www.afrobarometer.org/ (Accessed on October 12, 2022).

[10]   Akakandelwa A, Walubita G. Students' social media use and its perceived impact on their social life. A case study of the University of Zambia 2018.

[11]   Available From: https://gs.statcounter.com/ (Accessed on October 12, 2022).

[12]   Ahmad N, Naveed RT, Scholz M, Irfan M, Usman M, Ahmad I. CSR communication through social media: A litmus test for banking consumers' loyalty. Sustainability 2021; 13(4): 2319.
[http://dx.doi.org/10.3390/su13042319]

[13]   Stephen AT, Galak J. The effects of traditional and social earned media on sales: A study of a microlending marketplace. J Mark Res 2012; 49(5): 624-39.
[http://dx.doi.org/10.1509/jmr.09.0401]

[14]   Kotler P. Why broadened marketing has enriched marketing. AMS Rev 2018; 8(1-2): 20-2.
[http://dx.doi.org/10.1007/s13162-018-0112-4]

[15]   Voorveld HAM, Araujo T, Bernritter SF, Rietberg E, Vliegenthart R. How advertising in offline media drives reach of and engagement with brands on Facebook. Int J Advert 2018; 37(5): 785-805.
[http://dx.doi.org/10.1080/02650487.2018.1454703]

[16]   Djafarova E, Rushworth C. Exploring the credibility of online celebrities' Instagram profiles in influencing the purchase decisions of young female users. Comput Human Behav 2017; 68: 1-7.
[http://dx.doi.org/10.1016/j.chb.2016.11.009]

[17]   Kaplan AM, Haenlein M. Users of the world, unite! The challenges and opportunities of Social Media. Bus Horiz 2010; 53(1): 59-68.
[http://dx.doi.org/10.1016/j.bushor.2009.09.003]

[18]   Lee JE, Watkins B. YouTube vloggers' influence on consumer luxury brand perceptions and intentions. J Bus Res 2016; 69(12): 5753-60.
[http://dx.doi.org/10.1016/j.jbusres.2016.04.171]

[19]   Barnes NG, Mattson E. Social media in the 2009 Inc. 500: new tools and new trends. J New Commun Res 2009; 4(2): 70-9.

[20]   Coelho RLF, Oliveira DS, Almeida MIS. Does social media matter for post typology? Impact of post content on Facebook and Instagram metrics. Online Inf Rev 2016; 40(4): 458-71.
[http://dx.doi.org/10.1108/OIR-06-2015-0176]

[21]   Cvijikj I P, Michahelles F. Understanding the user generated content and interactions on a Facebook brand page. Intern J Soc Human Compu 2013; 14(2(1-2)): 118-40.

[22]   Katz E, Haas H, Gurevitch M. On the use of the mass media for important things. Am Sociol Rev 1973; 38(2): 164-81.
[http://dx.doi.org/10.2307/2094393]

[23]   Liu JH, North M, Li C. Relationship building through reputation and tribalism on companies' Facebook pages. Internet Res 2017; 27(5): 1149-69.
[http://dx.doi.org/10.1108/IntR-03-2016-0078]

[24]   Perse EM. Uses and gratifications. Oxford bibliographies in communication Retrieved from http://www oxfordbibliographies 2014.http://www. oxfordbibliographies. com/view/document/obo-9780199756841/obo-9780199756841-0132. xml

[25]   Awini G. Assessing the Impact of Social Media and Sports Fan Engagement: A Case of Accra Hearts of Oak and Kumasi Asante Kotoko 2019.

[26]   Thompson AJ, Martin AJ, Gee S, Geurin AN. Building brand and fan relationships through social media. Sport Bus Manag 2018; 8(3): 235-56.
[http://dx.doi.org/10.1108/SBM-04-2017-0024]

[27] Ellison NB, Steinfield C, Lampe C. Connection strategies: Social capital implications of Facebook-enabled communication practices. New Media Soc 2011; 13(6): 873-92.
[http://dx.doi.org/10.1177/1461444810385389]

[28] Peirce JW. PsychoPy—psychophysics software in Python. J Neurosci Methods 2007; 162(1-2): 8-13.
[http://dx.doi.org/10.1016/j.jneumeth.2006.11.017] [PMID: 17254636]

[29] Shao G. Understanding the appeal of user-generated media: a uses and gratification perspective. Internet Res 2009; 19(1): 7-25.
[http://dx.doi.org/10.1108/10662240910927795]

[30] Brodie RJ, Ilic A, Juric B, Hollebeek L. Consumer engagement in a virtual brand community: An exploratory analysis. J Bus Res 2013; 66(1): 105-14.
[http://dx.doi.org/10.1016/j.jbusres.2011.07.029]

[31] Vale L, Fernandes T. Social media and sports: driving fan engagement with football clubs on Facebook. J Strateg Mark 2018; 26(1): 37-55.
[http://dx.doi.org/10.1080/0965254X.2017.1359655]

[32] Knoll AH. Life on a Young Planet: The First Three Billion Years of Evolution on Earth-Updated Edition. Princeton University Press 2015; Vol. 35.
[http://dx.doi.org/10.1515/9781400866045]

[33] Slater SF. Developing a customer value-based theory of the firm. J Acad Mark Sci 1997; 25(2): 162-7.
[http://dx.doi.org/10.1007/BF02894352]

[34] Lavidge RJ, Steiner GA. A model for predictive measurements of advertising effectiveness. J Mark 1961; 25(6): 59-62.
[http://dx.doi.org/10.1177/002224296102500611]

[35] Griffiths JB. Colliding plane waves in general relativity. Courier Dover Publications 2016.

[36] Boyce C, Neale P. Conducting in-depth interviews: A guide for designing and conducting in-depth interviews for evaluation input . Pathfinder international.: Watertown, MA 2006.

[37] Flick U. Qualitative research designs Designing qualitative research 2007; 109-14.

[38] Maecker O, Barrot C, Becker JU. The effect of social media interactions on customer relationship management. Business Research 2016; 9(1): 133-55.
[http://dx.doi.org/10.1007/s40685-016-0027-6]

[39] Spotts HE, Purvis SC, Patnaik S. How digital conversations reinforce Super Bowl advertising: The power of earned media drives television engagement. J Advert Res 2014; 54(4): 454-68.
[http://dx.doi.org/10.2501/JAR-54-4-454-468]

CHAPTER 8

SMEs Use Artificial Intelligence in Africa: Benefits and Challenges

Alhassan Fatawu[1,*], **Abas S.**[1], **Stanley C.**[1] and **Susana A.**[2]

[1] *Tamale Technical University, Tamale-Ghana*

[2] *Accra Technical University, Accra-Ghana*

Abstract: Artificial Intelligence is a popular topic in digital transformation. Many books and articles have been written on the subject, although most of them cater to corporations rather than startups. The small and medium-sized businesses (SMEs) in Africa represent the economic backbone of the continent, so it is increasingly crucial that they have access to and can implement these technologies. This chapter provides a literature overview on the prevalence of AI in SMEs, discussing its current limits and its impact on enabling SMEs to reap its benefits. In the first place, we present an overview of the four AI tools and the enablers of AI. A thorough literature review is then performed on the difficulties associated with it . Finally, future trends and implications in research and development are summarized, along with future research topics for making AI an accessible technology to SMEs.

Keywords: AI, Automation, Internet, SMEs, Technology.

INTRODUCTION

When it comes to the Fourth Industrial Revolution (4IR) and the technologies it entails, small and medium-sized enterprises (SMEs) face unique difficulties around the world. This is due to a number of factors, such as difficulties obtaining credit and financing, lack of knowledge, lack of qualified labor, an inadequate digital infrastructure, and uncertainty about how to integrate advanced technology into business operations [1]. Artificial intelligence (AI) is no longer reserved for multinational corporations, and it seeks to inspire businesses of all sizes to take bold, well-considered steps toward integrating AI into their operations [1]. Since the turn of the millennium, gender-inclusive education, poverty reduction, and innovation at the level of individual businesses have all benefited greatly from the widespread use of the internet and other digital technologies [2]. Today's global economy and the fourth industrial revolution (also known as Industry 4.0) are

---

[*] **Corresponding author Alhassan Fatawu:** Tamale Technical University, Tamale-Ghana;
E-mail: alhassanfatawu29@yahoo.com

Mohammed Majeed, Abdul-Razak Abubakari, Awini Gideon and Jayadatta S. (Eds.)

indistinguishable from artificial intelligence (AI) [3-7]. Artificial intelligence (AI) is eliminating many enterprises' traditional sources of market advantage and redrawing the competitive borders of industries, thus rendering important resources and knowledge obsolete, and at the same time, a global race is underway [2, 8, 9].

Artificial intelligence (AI) has emerged as the go-to tool for resolving complicated business problems in many of the industries where SMEs are prevalent. Researchers spent a lot of time finding technological solutions to crucial business problems. However, additional facets of management have come to the fore as AI adoption, implementation, and use have increased [4]. Artificial intelligence is gaining traction around the world, which is changing how businesses compete and interact with their customers [10, 11]. However, the majority of the existing research on AI is geared toward large organizations and tends to focus on technical and commercial application rather than investigating the advantages of AI from a small and medium-sized enterprise (SME) viewpoint. This section provides a brief literature review that can be used by small and medium-sized enterprises (SMEs) for strategic AI deployment and for determining AI's actual value. This section's goal is to define the factors that encourage SMEs to adopt AI. This chapter summarizes and draws attention to the prospective research concerns within the scope of our study that could be investigated further.

Literature Review

AI

The term "artificial intelligence" describes the application of computers to do tasks typically associated with living organisms, such as pattern recognition, problem solving, and prediction [12]. Computerized systems using AI do cognitive tasks that humans typically handle [13]. With the help of AI, businesses are expected to be 40% more productive in 2035 than they are today [14]. This seems to be yet another requirement for competing on a worldwide scale [10]. Complementing one another, AI and ERP are viewed as crucial to participating in the 4IR [4]. By 2025, the artificial intelligence (AI) business might be worth $190 billion, and by 2027, that number could rise to $267 billion [15]. The impact of AI advancements on the business world is illustrated by the exponential expansion of this field. The private sector in Africa is no different. The private sector in Africa is innovating at the same rate or faster than the rest of the world [15]. Artificial intelligence (AI) is a group of technologies that allow machines to behave intelligently and mimic human senses, comprehension, and actions. Learning from experience and evolving over time both increase these capacities in humans.

To rephrase, AI allows robots to see their surroundings, form hypotheses about those surroundings, and even learn from experience in order to act in a manner appropriate to those surroundings and their underlying conditions. As AI systems improve in capability, they are being used in an increasing variety of business contexts [16]. According to McKinsey Global Institute [17], the retail, transportation and logistics, travel, automotive and assembly, and consumer packaged goods industries are prime candidates for the application of artificial intelligence to generate substantial value. Recent polls have shown that while the transportation, logistics, automotive, and technology industries have the highest percentage of AI adopters, process industries like chemicals have the lowest [3]. AI's primary functions include the detection of patterns, the acquisition of knowledge *via* experience, and the formulation of sound judgments without the need for a predetermined set of instructions. Several industries, such as transportation, banking, marketing and advertising, and even research, healthcare, security, and the public sector, are presenting rapid adoption of AI technology, as presented in the 2019 OECD report on Artificial Intelligence. AI systems can simulate complex, interdependent systems to enhance decision-making and cost-effectiveness in these industries, according to a study [18].

The rapidly evolving range of AI technologies has the ability to address some of the most critical issues faced by Sub-Saharan Africa and fuel development and expansion in essential industries. (1). Agricultural outputs will increase as a result of improved efficiency and effectiveness. In addition to this (2), people will have easier access to care that is both individualized and of greater quality. Thirdly, the influence of government services will increase as they become more efficient and user-friendly. Four, the accessibility and safety of financial services will increase, allowing more people to use them.

AI and SMEs

Industry is the key to the creation of a thriving AI ecosystem in Africa as the main developers of AI technology. From established players to entrepreneurs, startups, and SMEs, industry creates innovative products; provides invaluable knowledge, insight, and expertise to government for effective policymaking; and contributes to the development of local talent and skills for Africa's growing youthful population.

AI in Africa

Artificial intelligence (AI) systems are machine-based systems with varied degrees of autonomy that may, for a given set of human-defined objectives, generate predictions, suggestions, or judgments using large volumes of alternative data sources and data analytics [7]. As AI grows in popularity around the globe, a new AI ecosystem is blossoming in Africa. AI has the potential to aid in a wide range of areas in Africa, including but not limited to: poverty alleviation and education enhancement; the provision of healthcare and the elimination of disease; the resolution of sustainability issues; the fulfillment of the increasing demand for food resulting from the continent's rapid population growth; and the promotion of social inclusion. Access to new, productive technologies is what drives the growth Africa needs, and AI is making them more accessible than ever [4]. The Kenya-based non-profit Data Science Africa (DSA) has been working to spread awareness of the benefits of AI solutions across the continent since its inception in 2013. Through its summer schools and workshops, which have been hosted in Ethiopia, Ghana, Kenya, Nigeria, Tanzania, and Uganda, DSA provides a forum for AI practitioners and researchers across Africa to explore the growth and utility of AI.

Components of AI

Artificial intelligence (AI) can do the job better and faster than a human. The discipline of computer science known as artificial intelligence (AI) focuses on creating intelligent machines that can perform activities that normally require human intelligence. Automation, image/face recognition, NLP, data analytics, and predictive ability are some of AI's primary business uses. Machine learning, NLP, computer vision, and other related technologies are only a few of the many that make up the AI ecosystem. Advanced computing systems can now learn from experience, make predictions based on data, and even understand natural language [19].

Automation

Automation of scientific processes and identification of low-cost trials, for instance in the development of novel products, apparatus, or processes [18]. Intelligent automation driven by AI, on the other hand, is capable of finding solutions to issues in a wide variety of sectors, while traditional automation technology is task-specific. AI has the potential to automate tiresome processes/tasks without human intervention. Self-learning machines/software can also identify knowledge gaps and take corrective action thanks to intelligent automation. Unlike the automation assets of the past, which progressively degraded, the automation assets of today are constantly evolving and developing. Non-trivial jobs can now be automated with the help of modern AI systems. For small and medium-sized enterprises (SMEs), automation may boost productivity in a number of ways. Similarly, this kind of technology has the potential to aid small enterprises in reducing the effects of bureaucratic roadblocks and boosting their responsiveness. Automation enables predetermined system actions to be carried out at predetermined intervals. Intelligent automation refers to the automation of tasks in the physical environment that used to need human skills like problem-solving and obstacle navigation (Accenture, 2019). Some economic hubs in Sub-Saharan Africa have advanced digital infrastructure, access to money, and a cost-benefit analysis that leans toward automating their operations. Increased usage of automation technologies is anticipated, for example, in the high-wage and internationally competitive industrial sector and the high-wage service economy of sub-Saharan Africa [20]. Sub-Saharan Africa's expanding middle class in the formal economy stands to suffer greatly from the widespread adoption of automation technology. The 4th industrial revolution is predicated on the automation of employment, which is causing significant changes to the economies of developed, developing, and emerging nations alike. While some worry about widespread layoffs, others are more hopeful about the future of employment. The future is unpredictable, but we can gain insight into potential outcomes by analyzing the social, economic, regulatory, infrastructure, and capital variables that are either facilitating or impeding the automation revolution [20]. To emphasize, these elements vary from one country to the next, which means that the development and effects of automation will also vary.

Machine Learning

By simulating multiple layers of neural connectivity, deep learning neural networks are attempting to mimic the way real neurons communicate with one another in the brain [21]. Inspired by the way the human brain works, these models use multi-layer neural networks to learn and recognize complex patterns in data. Without the need to manually program any rules or specify any detectors, deep learning models may automatically recognize and classify data for use in further processing. These models can even discover previously unknown patterns (Krizhevsky, Sutskever & Hinton, 2017). It is theorized that such networks can operate at many generalization levels beginning with subfeatures and have a higher tolerance for background noise. Machine learning (ML) educates a computer to draw conclusions and make judgments from data [8]. To draw conclusions that don't require human judgment, it learns to spot trends and trends over time in previously collected data. Businesses can save time and effort thanks to automation that evaluates data and draws conclusions [22]. Machine learning (ML) is a subfield of artificial intelligence (AI) that explores the way in which software can "self-improve" by analyzing relevant datasets and acquiring new skills without being explicitly trained by human programmers [23].

Chatbots

Another well-known instance is the widespread use of AI chatbots in various sectors and on virtually every website we access today [8]. As a result, chatbots are now available to serve consumers both during and outside traditional business hours, alleviating pressure caused by a lack of human staff.

Deep Learning

One ML strategy is called "Deep Learning." Deep learning instructs a computer to use several layers of processing power to learn from data and provide accurate predictions [22]. Deep learning is a subfield of machine learning that acquires knowledge *via* the use of neural networks to process data [19]. What sets deep learning distinct is its ability to learn autonomously. Deep learning is more complicated than traditional machine learning, which is the key defining feature between the two. A deep learning model's variable relationships are used to describe this complexity. Deep learning problems involve a large number of fields of variables, which in turn leads to more intricate dependencies.

Neural Network

Deep learning is made possible by neural networks, which are computer systems loosely based on models of the neural connections in the human brain. Neural Networks are computational models that mimic the way human brain cells function. In essence, they are a set of algorithms designed to mimic the way the human brain processes information by identifying patterns in data and learning from experience. What sets deep learning apart from machine learning is its increased complexity. The intricate nature of the interdependence of variables is captured by deep learning. Neural networks are a subfield of AI that draws inspiration from neuroscience while also including cognitive science and automated task execution (a part of biology that concerns the nerve and nervous system of the human brain). Because the human brain has an endless number of neurons, a neural network attempts to codify these neurons into a system or computer.

Computer Vision

AI uses a wide variety of resources to mimic human intelligence and duplicate it using different algorithms on different platforms. It is *via* the process of image recognition in machine learning that the field of computer vision, which studies the ability of computers to analyze and understand visual data, has emerged. Algorithms in computer vision attempt to interpret images by analyzing their constituent pieces. As a result, the machine is better able to learn from its observations and categorize a given batch of photos [8]. The field of computer vision makes use of deep learning and pattern recognition to decipher visual data (such as charts, tables, PDF images, and videos) [19].

Robots in AI

Even before artificial intelligence was possible, progress was being made in robotics. At this time, AI is speeding up robotics' ability to develop new, useful robots. Artificially intelligent robots are now being used in a wide variety of fields, from manufacturing to packing. Examples of how AI is being used with robots include (1) real-time course correction using AI and improved vision systems, and (2) in-process learning of the optimal route for a given task using AI [8]. Robots are frequently used to accomplish jobs that would be too demanding for humans to carry out consistently. The automotive assembly line and heavy lifting are two of the most common applications of robotics. Robotics is a multidisciplinary field that draws upon many other scientific and technological disciplines in addition to mechanical and electrical engineering. The robotics field governs every aspect of robot creation, operation, and application. It focuses on the use of computers for managerial purposes, the production of intelligent results, and the transformation of data.

Fuzzy Logic

They provide relevant flexibility for thinking, which leads to inaccuracies and uncertainties of any condition, which is necessary in the actual world when it can be difficult to determine whether the condition is true or not. Fuzzy logic, in its simplest form, is a method for representing and modifying uncertain information through the use of a degree of correctness measure. Concepts whose veracity is inherently hazy can be reasoned about using fuzzy logic [24]. It is easy and versatile to use machine learning methods with fuzzy logic, and these methods can help approximate human logic. It is just a broader application of traditional logic, in which an idea has a truth value between zero and one. According to accepted logic, a value of 1.0 is assigned to a fully true idea, whereas a value of 0.0 is assigned to a fully false one. In contrast, fuzzy logic allows for a value that is neither fully true nor false.

Cognitive Computing

Cognitive computing algorithms (Brain-Computer Interfaces) attempt to produce the intended result by analyzing text, audio, images, and objects in the same way as a human brain does [8]. The ultimate goal of cognitive computing is to simulate human reasoning in a digital environment. Understanding human language and the significance of visuals is at the heart of this initiative, which aims to mimic and enhance human-machine interaction [19].

Image/face Recognition

Image recognition is the process of determining an image's category and locating things of interest within it. There is a great deal of overlap between the concepts of image recognition, photo recognition, and picture recognition. A facial recognition system uses artificial intelligence to map a person's facial traits from a picture, which is then compared to a database to identify a match. Companies that build smartphones utilize facial recognition technology (to unlock the device) and social media platforms (to identify users in uploaded photos so they may be tagged) use the technology for a variety of purposes. However, there are significant privacy concerns with such systems because data can be acquired without the user's knowledge or consent. Based on how humans recognize items in varying image sets, image recognition is a process used to identify objects inside an image and classify them into certain categories. Another prominent topic that is gaining traction right now is the use of AI for picture recognition; this subfield of AI is projected to generate almost USD 39 billion in revenue by 2021 [25]. As a broad field, computer vision makes extensive use of deep learning for a variety of tasks, including but not limited to: image processing, image classification, object recognition, object segmentation, image coloring, picture reconstruction, and synthesis. To automate tasks that the human visual system is capable of, computer vision involves programming computers to acquire a high level of understanding from input digital images or video [25].

Natural Language Processing

Natural language processing (NLP) is a method for teaching computers how to read, analyze, and create written and spoken language [19]. NLP, or natural language processing, is the branch of AI and computer science that enables machines to understand and interact with human speech. It is a method for using computers to analyze human speech. It is the software that lets computers read and comprehend text much like people do. Natural language processing (NLP) is the study of how computers read, comprehend, and interpret human language. The system will respond appropriately once it has recognized the user's intent [22]. Natural language processing (NLP) is a methodology focused on generating information from textual input through search and analysis. NLP libraries are used by programmers to train computers to parse text for relevant information. Common applications of natural language processing include determining whether an email is spam by analyzing its text and subject line [24]. Users who lack the time to fully master a new language will find Natural Language

Processing (NLP) to be an invaluable tool. Actually, Natural Language Processing (NLP) is a branch of AI and linguistics that focuses on teaching computers to decipher human-written text. It was developed in response to the need for a more natural method of user-computer interaction [26].

Data Analytics

Business, manufacturing, and end-user data analytics for better efficiency and output [18]. Analytical work entails seeking out, comprehending, and conveying insights hidden inside datasets. Therefore, the goal of Analytical AI is to aid in data-driven decision making by uncovering previously unseen insights, patterns, correlations, or dependencies in data. As a result, it has become an integral aspect of artificial intelligence, used in the field of modern business intelligence to provide insights about an organization and provide suggestions or recommendations *via* analytical processing. An analytical AI model can be constructed using a number of machine learning and deep learning approaches to address a specific practical issue. A data-driven analytical model, for instance, is used to evaluate potential threats to your company [22].

Predictive Capacity

Prototyping, cost estimation, and design optimization would all benefit greatly from the addition of 3D printing [9]. Neural network-based machine learning models for prediction have proven to be quite effective in evaluating enormous data sets. Middle management in SMEs must strike a continual balance between meeting operational needs and preserving financial reserves. There is a growing amount of uncertainty in the world, but AI can help them with this work by allowing them to make more precise and effective projections further out in the future, on timescales of weeks to months. Businesses can save money on unused assets thanks to AI's ability to maximize resource utilization. Through automated, need-based resource allocation, AI with predictive capacity can greatly improve resource use.

Impact of AI on SMEs in Africa

With AI, the cost of producing predictions can be drastically reduced, and selecting choices is made much simpler. Small and medium-sized enterprises (SMEs) can use predictive analytics to improve asset management, automate business projections using real-time data, and reduce their risk exposure. Additionally, improved forecasting power paves the way for more precise market segmentation and provides small and medium-sized enterprises with fresh avenues for innovation [27]. AI was developed to supplement human capacities and guide us in making complex choices with far-reaching ramifications. From a technical perspective, that's the correct response. From a philosophical standpoint, AI has the potential to enable people to lead more fulfilling lives without having to engage in manual labor, and to aid in the management of the complex web of interconnected individuals, businesses, states, and nations so that they can work together for the good of all humanity.

Artificial intelligence (AI) has broad potential applications across a variety of industries, from the service and low-tech sectors to the full gamut of corporate processes, from planning to execution. Artificial intelligence has the potential to significantly improve several business processes, including marketing, sales, supply chain management, and production [13]. In the retail sector, transportation and logistics services, and the automotive and assembly manufacturing industries, among others, AI has the potential to make a substantial impact on value creation. Artificial intelligence (AI) systems rely heavily on learning. Learning, in this context, refers to the theoretical capability of AI computer systems to acquire new information and refine their existing understanding based on their observations and previous encounters. In order to predict the outcomes of incoming inputs, AI algorithms evaluate a dataset consisting of input-output pairs for a particular function [19].

Artificial intelligence (AI) can have a significant impact on the business environment of small and medium-sized enterprises (SMEs) by making government agencies, courts, and tax authorities more efficient, cutting down on bureaucracy, protecting the integrity of the internet's backbone, facilitating easier access to financing, streamlining the process of matching workers with open positions, and lowering the price tag of R&D [28]. The risk of (presumably) large enterprises maintaining profits and prices above a reasonable competitive level, to the detriment of smaller businesses, is also raised by the use of algorithms in the market place.

AI has the potential to improve the effectiveness of asset management and maintenance. Foreseeing when and where an asset may fail allows for preventative maintenance to be performed on its components. IoT sensors continuously monitor asset health, and this data, along with information gathered from the asset's previous life cycle, is used to make diagnoses about the asset's current health and spot any anomalies. Predictive maintenance offers significant advantages over reactive maintenance by decreasing the likelihood of downtime (and thus the expense of production or business interruption in the event of an interruption) and eliminating the need for routine maintenance [8]. In the service industries, such as retail and hospitality, robots equipped with artificial intelligence are being employed to assist customers. These robots use NLP to have natural, human-like conversations with clients. Using machine learning, these systems improve the more they engage with humans [8]. AI allows for more efficient, accurate, and inexpensive packing. In the end, it facilitates the easy installation and relocation of robotic systems by recording and continuously refining specific robot motions.

Benefits of SMEs Adopting AI

The adoption of Artificial Intelligence (AI) can bring numerous benefits to Small and Medium-sized Enterprises (SMEs). Here are some of the key advantages:

Improved Decision Making: AI can analyze large amounts of data quickly and accurately, providing valuable insights that can help SMEs make informed business decisions. This can lead to improved operational efficiency, better resource allocation, and increased profitability.

Increased Productivity: AI can automate routine tasks, freeing up employees to focus on more complex and value-added activities. This can lead to increased productivity and efficiency.

Enhanced Customer Experience: AI can be used to personalize the customer experience, from providing tailored product recommendations to offering 24/7 customer service through AI-powered chatbots. This can lead to improved customer satisfaction and loyalty.

Better Risk Management: AI can help SMEs identify and manage risks more effectively. For example, AI can be used to detect fraudulent transactions in real-time or predict potential supply chain disruptions.

Innovation and New Business Opportunities: AI can enable SMEs to innovate and create new business opportunities. For example, AI can be used to develop new products or services, or to enter new markets.

Cost Savings: By automating tasks, improving efficiency, and reducing errors, AI can lead to significant cost savings for SMEs.

Competitive Advantage: By leveraging AI, SMEs can gain a competitive advantage over businesses that are slower to adopt this technology.

However, it is important to note that while AI can bring many benefits, it also comes with challenges, such as the need for technical expertise, data privacy concerns, and the risk of job displacement. Therefore, SMEs need to carefully consider these factors when deciding to adopt AI.

Challenges of SMEs Adopting AI

Some of the challenges that small and medium-sized enterprises (SMEs) encounter in implementing AI are shared by other digital technologies, such as a lack of knowledge and preparedness, while others are unique to machine learning and its implementation.

The media and public attention paid to the small and medium-sized enterprise (SME) sector's adoption of artificial intelligence in Finland and Sweden sped up the transition to AI (Savola *et al.*, 2018). Small and medium-sized enterprises (SMEs) have greater challenges than major corporations when trying to implement AI technology due to a lack of standardized business procedures, structured approaches to innovation, and sufficient managerial expertise [29]. The quality of an AI system is only as good as the data it is trained on. As we delve deeper into the world of AI, the inherent bias introduced by the data becomes more and more apparent. Racism, sexism, communalism, and ethnic prejudices are all forms of bias. Algorithms can now do a lot of the heavy lifting in modern society, deciding who gets a loan or a job. Bad, unjust, and unethical outcomes are possible if the algorithms responsible for making such pivotal judgments have acquired biases over time [19]. Consequences, such as governments' failure to ensure citizens' data security and privacy and to mitigate the impact of cyber and national security, may come from Africa's general lack of institutional capacity and an AI regulatory framework. Cybersecurity has been an issue since the 3rd Industrial Revolution (3IR), but the advancements brought about by AI and IoT further complicate both individual and national security by connecting vital and potentially life-saving devices *via* wireless networks [30].

Inexact benefits and high prices of AI: It still takes a lot of time and money to build and maintain an AI system. Labeling a single hour of footage, for instance, can take up to eight hours [31]. Small and medium-sized enterprises (SMEs) may not have the cash flow or financial resources to absorb the capital requirements associated with establishing an AI system, despite the fact that open-source AI tools are available and the training costs of AI algorithms are decreasing [32]. In addition, the price of gaining access to financing can be increased by factors such as uncertainty and the absence of concrete evidence and business strategies [18].

Social ramifications, leadership influence, decision-making methodology, and policy paralysis were all obstacles to AI adoption [33]. Lack of persistent efforts, lack of prioritization, and lack of qualified resources were identified by Walczak [24] as three of the most significant barriers to AI adoption. Black boxes best describe AI algorithms. Very little is known about how AI algorithms function on the inside. In the case of a predicting system, for instance, we know what the prediction is but not how it was determined [19]. Because of this, AI is not completely dependable.

CASE STUDY

Company Background

The company in focus is a small to medium-sized enterprise (SME) in the retail sector based in Nairobi, Kenya. The company has a diverse product range and caters to a broad customer base across the country. With the advent of e-commerce, the company also operates an online store, which has significantly increased its reach and customer base.

AI Implementation

Recognizing the potential of AI, the company decided to implement AI-based solutions for inventory management and customer targeting. For inventory management, the company used an AI-powered system that could predict the demand for different products based on historical sales data, current market trends, and seasonal factors. The system was able to optimize inventory levels, reducing the risk of overstocking or understocking, and thereby minimizing storage costs and potential lost sales. For customer targeting, the company used an AI-based recommendation engine on its online store. The system analyzed customers' browsing and purchasing behavior to recommend products that they might be interested in. This not only improved the shopping experience for customers but also increased the company's sales and customer retention rate.

Challenges Faced

The company faced several challenges during the implementation of these AI solutions. Firstly, there was a lack of in-house expertise in AI, which meant that the company had to rely on external vendors for implementation. Secondly, the company had to ensure that the AI systems complied with data protection regulations, which required additional investment in data security measures. Lastly, there was some resistance from staff who were concerned about the potential impact of AI on their jobs.

Outcomes Achieved

Despite these challenges, the company was able to successfully implement AI solutions and achieve significant benefits. The AI-powered inventory management system reduced storage costs by 20% and lost sales due to out-of-stock items by 15%. The AI-based recommendation engine increased online sales by 30% and customer retention rate by 10%. Furthermore, the company was able to upskill its staff to work with the AI systems, thereby alleviating their concerns and enhancing their capabilities.

CONCLUSION

This case study demonstrates the potential of AI for SMEs in the retail sector. Despite the challenges, the benefits achieved by the company in terms of cost savings, increased sales, and improved customer retention highlight the value of AI. However, it also underscores the importance of addressing staff concerns and ensuring data protection when implementing AI solutions.

DISCUSSION

The world's SMEs have been quick to adopt AI and other cutting-edge technologies, but they've also seen a number of obstacles in their adoption [7, 15, 17]. However, most African countries still confront governance challenges and lack of institutional capacity, limiting their ability to construct enabling institutional and technological infrastructure for AI development and implementation. The topic of what policies and approaches for institutional development should be adopted to assist artificial intelligence (AI) start-ups in Africa is raised by this leadership challenge. The yawning chasm in Africa's social standing is exacerbated by the continent's lagging technological development [34]. When it comes to AI, Deep Learning (DL) is important. As a well-known topic of study in the field of machine learning, DL is not an easy task. When it comes to facial recognition, deep learning gives SMEs the ability to achieve higher-level accuracy than is possible with conventional AI approaches.

IMPLICATION

As a technology that bridges the gap between machines and humans, AI has the potential to reshape many facets of human contribution to the industrial sector. The adoption of new technologies presents both industry and society with significant hurdles. Product innovation, product portfolios, and customer habits are just a few of the many spheres of influence that will be impacted. This study's findings have implications for the SME industry in Africa and other similar countries, broadening our understanding of the topic. These findings may aid Industry and societal decision-makers in making a well-informed choice about AI deployment, which is especially important given the SME sector's centrality to the global economy.

As the report included data on the implementation of emerging disruptive technologies like AI, which might assist in reducing company failure, its potential ramifications for social change went far beyond the SME sector in Africa. The results of this research would benefit the SME sector, boost the performance of the Industry as a whole, and help make sustainable development a reality. Small and medium-sized enterprises (SMEs) that embrace AI are better positioned to develop innovative products that address pressing societal issues like food insecurity, pollution, and slowing economic growth. The use of AI improves the quality, velocity, and precision of any task. Important uses include fraud detection and prevention, improved credit scoring, and the automation of labor-intensive data administration tasks. Aside from facilitating the development of novel solutions to challenges that are too difficult to tackle manually, artificial intelligence enhances the process across sectors and applications.

FUTURE OF ARTIFICIAL INTELLIGENCE

Market penetration of driverless cars is predicted to increase significantly as more and more automakers continue to invest in autonomous vehicles. Statista predicts that by 2022, the worldwide market for autonomous vehicles is worth approximately $146.4 billion, up sharply from the $105.7 billion recorded in 2021 [28]. Humans have always been intrigued by the possibilities presented by new technologies and works of fiction, and we are currently experiencing a period of unprecedented progress. The field of artificial intelligence is poised to be the next revolutionary step in technological development. In the fields of AI and ML, companies all around the world are developing ground-breaking new technologies. Not only is AI changing the course of every sector and every person's life, but it is also the primary impetus behind other developing technologies like big data, robots, and the Internet of Things. As a result of its rapid expansion, it is likely to remain a leader in technical development for the foreseeable future. As a result, the job market is ripe with possibilities for those who have the necessary education and credentials. The development of these technologies promises to have a growing influence on our culture and standard of living. These days, you may utilize your face to speed up security checks and make everyone more aware at the airport. Major airports are starting to implement this method due to the rising popularity of high-resolution 3D facial recognition, thermal facial recognition technology, and image recognition models.

CONCLUSION

As they grow in size and sophistication, artificial intelligence systems become more powerful. Researchers in the field of artificial intelligence (AI) are always working to develop new software systems for use in areas as varied as speech recognition, natural language processing, automated learning, and knowledge. Corporations are increasingly putting their faith in AI to make important judgments as it spreads throughout all facets of business. Artificial intelligence (AI) is now widely used in a wide variety of contexts, from increasing business profits to improving customer experiences. The availability of AI, ML, deep learning, and neural networks has made this transition to AI feasible, not just for large corporations but also for SMEs. Africa stands to benefit greatly from advancements in artificial intelligence. Today's small and medium-sized enterprises (SMEs) rely heavily on human cognition to deliver individualized services and make timely, data-driven decisions. The adoption of AI was uneven across many different types of businesses. AI has the potential to be a catalyst for economic growth, social progress, and political democratization if governments can successfully navigate the risks involved. Opportunities in agriculture, healthcare, financial services, and public services—all crucial to Africa's development—could be greatly increased. Artificial intelligence (AI) will help employees, entrepreneurs, and enterprises compete on a global scale and in the vanguard of economic innovation by providing them with access to cutting-edge digital tools. Academics, professionals, and governments all around the world are trying to comprehend the ramifications of AI and the ways in which its growth may be fostered because of its predicted contribution and impact on future economies. However, there is still a vast divide between the Global North and South when it comes to AI development and implementation. If this gap is not overcome, it has the potential to exacerbate existing inequities. To this end, governments in several African nations, including Algeria, Egypt, Ghana, Kenya, Nigeria, and South Africa, have set up ministries and agencies charged with developing national AI strategies to facilitate the introduction of AI into industries, economies, educational systems, agricultural practices, and physical infrastructure.

However, strong policy solutions are needed to overcome the barriers on the road. Adjustments in the workplace and in business will need to be made, and new ethical problems raised by AI will need careful consideration. There are additional difficulties in Africa, such as a lack of connectivity, unprepared educational institutions, and a dearth of digital data, which aggravate the already existing difficulties in the labor market and ethical considerations. Africa must take bold measures to overcome its unique problems if it is to have any hope of catching up to the countries that have already begun to make strides in artificial intelligence development. Whilst it is true that AI has the potential to replace humans in a variety of occupations, there's also a chance that we'll see a rise in human-machine collaboration in the next years, which would help both parties' cognitive abilities and lead to greater productivity.

RECOMMENDATION FOR SMEs OWNERS IN AFRICA

Small and medium-sized enterprises (SMEs) might outsource the creation of AI applications to third-party developers in order to save money and time. The level of intensity and maturity of the SME transformation varies between fully autonomous development of AI models and no adoption at all [27]. One step that small and medium-sized enterprises (SMEs) can take is to work toward creating a unified data pool by eliminating data silos between departments. Consumer, user, production, or administrative data collected by SMEs can form the basis for structured and time-series datasets that can be used to create value through the use of AI [17]. Improving SMEs' data readiness now may help them be better prepared to use machine learning techniques with their workflows if they become more cost-effective.

ADVICE FOR AFRICAN GOVERNMENTS

Public-private partnerships (PPPs) are an effective model for financing and constructing infrastructure in Africa, and the continent's governments should think about pursuing them. PPPs help governments access resources and important expertise from local and international partners, while also better aligning private investment with public policy objectives through risk management. The number of public-private partnerships (PPPs) in the Sub-Saharan area is low and underdeveloped compared to other markets. Most PPP projects in the region are focused on just a few countries (South Africa, Nigeria, Kenya, and Uganda), and these are all in the renewable energy field. To lessen the impact of automation on employment, it is also important to retrain the current workforce and adapt educational systems to meet the demands of new digital occupations. To help more people become aware of AI's benefits and to provide young people with skills relevant to the 4IR, it might be integrated into the curriculum of elementary and secondary schools. More people being aware of AI opportunities, increasing its usage, and creating a pipeline of skills to compete in the upcoming future of work would reduce worries about AI entrenching inequities if such practice were to become popular across Africa. Policymakers may want to think about instituting some minimum standards or best practices for data management in AI-based methods. As an example, these might include data quality, the sufficiency of the dataset utilized, and other factors relevant to the application of the AI model, as well as protections that give confidence in the model's robustness with respect to avoiding biases. Best practices to reduce the possibility of discrimination include performing appropriate sense checks of model results against baseline datasets and other tests based on whether protected classes may be inferred from other attributes in the data.

Protection of sensitive information: Individuals are more likely to use AI-based solutions that rely on their data if they are confident in the framework protecting their data privacy and security. The goal of data privacy and security legislation should be to keep users' information safe while not impeding the free flow of information across borders. To increase access to cutting-edge technology, governments should implement digital strategies and policies that promote widespread cloud usage. It is within the power of African governments to make AI's promise a reality for their people. There are significant obstacles to be overcome, but there is also an opportunity to leapfrog competitors by drawing on the expertise of countries that are already at the forefront of artificial intelligence. Better data governance by financial sector corporations is an area where policymakers may focus their attention to better safeguard consumers across all financial AI applications. Data privacy and confidentiality, data concentration and its potential impact on the competitive dynamics of the market, as well as the risk of unintended bias and discrimination against subsets of the population, and data drifts, are all concerns raised in this note that are related to data management. When it comes to defining a model's ability to preserve its predictive powers in tail event settings, the relevance of data is as undeniable as it is when it comes to training, testing, and validating ML models [29].

FUTURE STUDIES

Due to the high cost of implementing AI technology, it may not be applicable to Microenterprises, which are often run on a small scale and in a simple environment, and which have no use for complex information technology infrastructure. We suggest, however, that future research pays special attention to such organizations, as they may hold the key to uncovering new, cost-effective ways to harness technology.

REFERENCES

[1]   The Tokenisation of Assets and Potential Implications for Financial Markets 2020. Available From: https://www.oecd.org/finance/The-Tokenisation-of-Assets-and-Potential-Implications-forFinancial-Markets.htm

[2]   DSA: About data science africa (2020). Data Science Africa. Available from: http://www.datascienceafrica.org/

[3]   Boston Consulting Group. AI in the factory of the future: The ghost in the machine 2018. Available From: https://www.bcg.com/publications/2018/artificial-intelligence-factory-future.

[4]   Haddara M, Elragal A. The Readiness of ERP Systems for the Factory of the Future. Procedia Comput Sci 2015; 64: 721-8.
       [http://dx.doi.org/10.1016/j.procs.2015.08.598]

[5]   Hila M. Artificial Intelligence for Citizen Services and Government, Harvard Kennedy School ASH Centre for Democratic Governance and Innovation. 2017.

[6]   Initial Coin Offerings (ICOs) for SME Financing 2019. Available from: https://www.

oecd.org/finance/initial-coin-offerings-for-sme-financing.htm (accessed on 16 September 2020).

[7]   What is Artificial Intelligence in 2023? Types, Trends, and Future of it? 2022. Available from: https://www.mygreatlearning.com/blog/what-is-artificial-intelligence/

[8]   Scoping the OECD AI principles: Deliberations of the Expert Group on Artificial Intelligence at the OECD. AIGO 2019.

[9]   Makridakis S. The forthcoming Artificial Intelligence (AI) revolution: Its impact on society and firms. Futures 2017; 90: 46-60.
[http://dx.doi.org/10.1016/j.futures.2017.03.006]

[10]   OECD Business and Finance Outlook 2020: Sustainable and Resilient Finance. Paris: OECD Publishing 2020.

[11]   Jiang F, Jiang Y, Zhi H, *et al.* Artificial intelligence in healthcare: past, present and future. Stroke Vasc Neurol 2017; 2(4): 230-43.
[http://dx.doi.org/10.1136/svn-2017-000101] [PMID: 29507784]

[12]   Algorithms and Collusion: Competition Policy in the Digital Age 2017. Available From: https://www.oecd.org/daf/competition/Algorithms-and-colllusion-competition-policy-in-thedigital-age.pdf

[13]   The Impact of Big Data and Artificial Intelligence (AI) in the Insurance Sector 2020. Available From: https://www.oecd.org/finance/Impact-Big-Data-AI-in-the-Insurance-Sector.htm

[14]   Africa CEO Forum. How to accelerate AI adoption among African companies? Available From https://www.theafricaceoforum.com/en/ressources/comment-favoriser-ladoption-de-lia-par-les-ente-reprises-africaines-%E2%80%AF%E2%80%AF/ (accessed on: Jan. 3, 2020).

[15]   Scott C. How UK Banks are looking to use AI and machine learning. Computer world UK 2017.

[16]   Noted from the AI frontier: Insights from hundreds of use cases 2018. Company, Available From: https://www.mckinsey.com/~/media/mckinsey/featured%20insights/artificial%20intelligence/notes%20from%20the%20ai%20frontier%20applications%20and%20value%20of%20deep%20learning/notes-from-the-ai-frontier-insights-from-hundreds-of-use-cases-discussion-paper (Accessed on 16 December 2019).

[17]   Artificial Intelligence in Society. Paris: OECD Publishing 2019.

[18]   Kanade V. What Is Artificial Intelligence (AI)? Definition, Types, Goals, Challenges, and Trends in 2022. 2022.https://www.spiceworks.com/tech/artificial-intelligence/articles/what-is-ai/

[19]   Gaus A, Hoxtell W. Automation and the Future of Work in Sub-Saharan Africa. Berlin: KonradAdenauer-Stiftung 2019.

[20]   OECD Business and Finance Outlook 2019: Strengthening Trust in Business. Paris: OECD Publishing 2019.

[21]   Sarker I H. Deep learning: a comprehensive overview on techniques, taxonomy, applications and research directions. SN Comput Sci 2021; 2(6): 1-20.

[22]   Sarker IH. Machine learning: algorithms, real-world applications and research directions. SN Computer Science 2021; 2(3): 160.
[http://dx.doi.org/10.1007/s42979-021-00592-x] [PMID: 33778771]

[23]   Tyagi N. 6 Major Branches of Artificial Intelligence (AI) 2020. https://www.analyticssteps.com/blogs/6-major-branches-artificial-intelligence-ai

[24]   Lisowski E. 2022.https://addepto.com/blog/using-artificial-intelligence-ai-for-image-recognition/

[25]   Khurana D, Koli A, Khatter K, Singh S. Natural language processing: state of the art, current trends and challenges. Multimedia Tools Appl 2022.
[http://dx.doi.org/10.1007/s11042-022-13428-4] [PMID: 35855771]

[26]   Artificial intelligence: Changing landscape for SMEs 2023. Available From:https://www.oecd-ilibrary.org/sites/01a4ae9den/index.html?itemId=/content/ component/

[27]   OECD SME and Entrepreneurship Outlook 2019. Paris: OECD Publishing 2019.

[28]   Brynjolfsson E, Mcafee A. The business of artificial intelligence. Harvard Business Review 2017; 7: 3-11.

[29]   Wilner AS. Cybersecurity and its discontents: Artificial intelligence, the Internet of Things, and digital misinformation. Int J 2018; 73(2): 308-16.
[http://dx.doi.org/10.1177/0020702018782496]

[30]   Murgia M. AI's new workforce: The data-labelling industry spreads globally 2019. Available From: https://www.ft.com/content/56dde36c-aa40-11e9-984c-fac8325aaa04 (accessed on 5 May 2020).

[31]   Coleman C, *et al.* DAWNBench: An End-to-End Deep Learning Benchmark and Competition 2020. Available From: https://dawn.cs.stanford.edu/benchmark/#imagenet-train-cost (accessed on 4 March 2020).

[32]   Alsheibani S, Cheung Y, Messom C. Artificial intelligence adoption: AIreadiness at firm-level. In PACIS 2018; 37.

[33]   Artificial Intelligence, Machine Learning and Big Data in Finance Opportunities, Challenges, and Implications for Policy Makers 2021. Available From: https://www.oecd.org/finance/artificial-intelligence-machine-learningbig-data-in-finance.htm

[34]   Walczak S. Artificial Neural Networks and other AI Applications for Business Management Decision Support. Int J Sociotechnology Knowl Dev 2016; 8(4): 1-20.
[http://dx.doi.org/10.4018/IJSKD.2016100101]

SUBJECT INDEX

T

V

W

www.ingramcontent.com/pod-product-compliance
Lightning Source LLC
Chambersburg PA
CBHW041708210326
41598CB00007B/578